# The Boom Bap Review

## VOLUME 4: 2022

MC Till

Donald "Profound" DeVold

Beau Brown

Michael Stover

marcus (iomos marad) singleton

Joe "Joe November" Thomas

Proofreading by Joe Thomas & MC Till

Additional Proofreading by Karyn Exilus

Cover Artwork by Phat Hentoff

Licensed by Creative Commons © 2022 Everybody's Hip Hop
Some rights reserved.
ISBN: 9798363801730

# DEDICATIONS

To Phife, Paten Locke, Tame One, Hurricane G and all of us who feel the loss of friends and family. May we find comfort in beautiful things like music.

To iomos marad whose presence is all over this book even though his words are not. He is finishing up a doctoral program. We are proud of you and the work you are doing. Keep pushing!

To Big Sto. Your team at Everybody's Hip-Hop sees you and your work. You are invaluable. Without you, we would have never started this series.

# TABLE OF CONTENTS

|  |  | Introductory Stuff | 1 |
|---|---|---|---|
| **Pt 1** | | **The Top 100** | **3** |
| | 1 | Albums 1-30 | 6 |
| | 2 | Albums 31-50 | 37 |
| | 3 | Albums 51-100+ | 44 |
| | | Honorable Mentions | 63 |
| | | Super Short EPs and other Spectacular Things | 64 |
| **Pt 2** | | **Long-Form Reviews** | **65** |
| | 4 | *Glory in the Weight* – Tab-One | 66 |
| | 5 | *Four Finger Ring* – The Bad Seed | 69 |
| | 6 | *Magic* – Nas | 73 |
| | 7 | *Sheep Stu* – Dres & Stu Bangas | 76 |
| | 8 | *Acres of Diamonds* – Ill Conscious & Mute Won | 78 |
| | 9 | *The Sundown E.P.* – Th.iii.rd & Freddie Marr | 81 |
| | 10 | *Set Out in the Dark* – Mighty Theodore | 84 |
| | 11 | *Omowale* – Wildchild | 87 |
| **Pt 3** | | **An Essay, Some Liner Notes, and a Dedication** | **91** |
| | 12 | *Who You Callin' a B\*\*\*h?* | 92 |
| | 13 | Liner Notes with Tone Spliff | 95 |
| | 14 | Liner Notes with Ghettosocks & DK | 98 |
| | 15 | Liner Notes with Awon | 101 |
| | 16 | Liner Notes with Mattic | 108 |
| | 17 | Paten Locke Tribute by Dillon Maurer | 120 |
| **Pt 4** | | **Retrospectives** | **123** |
| | 18 | 35 Years Later \| *Paid in Full* – Eric B & Rakim | 124 |
| | 19 | 30 Years Later \| *The Predator* – Ice Cube / *The Chronic* – Dr. Dre | 127 |
| | 20 | 30 Years Later \| *Bizarre Ride II the Pharcyde* – The Pharcyde | 131 |
| | 21 | 25 Years Later \| *Jewelz* – O.C. | 134 |

| | | |
|---|---|---|
| 22 | 25 Years Later \| *Doom* – Mood | 137 |
| 23 | 25 Years Later \| *Fan-tas-tic Vol. 1* – Slum Village | 139 |
| 24 | 20 Years Later \| *Power in Numbers* – Jurassic 5 | 143 |
| 25 | 20 Years Later \| *Blazing Arrow* – Blackalicious | 146 |
| 26 | 15 Years Later \| *Below the Heavens* – Blu & Exile | 149 |
| 27 | 10 Years Later \| *Cancer 4 Cure* – El-P / *R.A.P. Music* – Killer Mike | 152 |
| 28 | 5 Years Later \| *Return of the Don* – Kool G. Rap | 155 |
| **Pt 5** | **The People's Lists** | **159** |
| 29 | Fhaez | 160 |
| 30 | Ismail Ghedamsi-filion | 161 |
| | Some Final Stuff | 163 |

# INTRODUCTORY STUFF

Here we are at our fourth *Boom Bap Review*. A lot has happened since we launched our first book back in the fall of 2019. Many of us have suffered immeasurable loss. My wife lost her dad around the release date of that first book while I lost my father just a few months later in 2020. The pandemic came and went and came again. Maybe we are still in it. Maybe not. A recession hit us. Well, it is going to. Or maybe it did already depending on who you ask. We experienced political unrest, riots in the streets, peaceful protests, and a deadly attempt to take over Congress and upend a democratic election. And most of what I just expressed happened here in the United States. This isn't taking into account the wars and other atrocities that have happened all across the world. People do evil things and the world seems to be dying along with many of its institutions and inhabitants.

Yet, here we are. Beauty doesn't give up. Like 2Pac's rose rising up through the concrete, somehow we figure out how to capture what's beautiful about humanity. Even finding a way to express the burdens of this life through art can be breathtaking. Skyzoo, Pharoahe Monch, and many others did it last year. This year, artists like The Bad Seed, Tab-One, Black Thought, and countless others gave us similar experiences where we could soar above this world's ills and taste heaven, even if it's just a sip.

So again I say here we are. You might feel incredible, fending off any and all negativity coming your way or trying to. You might not even see anything negative and are currently experiencing a bit of bliss. Alternatively, you might feel the weight of the world, the entirety of it. You might feel like the simple task of breathing just feels like a little too much right now. Well, if you dig boom bap Hip-Hop, I suggest there is a beautiful rose just beneath your feet. You might not see it yet, but the roots are there. Give yourself an hour or so and jump into some of the titles we offer you in this book. May they celebrate your highs and lift you at your lows.

Then, if you like what you hear, go find the artists' Bandcamp sites and buy their music. You can be their rose:)

Enjoy.

MC Till

# Part One
# THE TOP 100

# How we selected the top 100

I (MC Till) promise this top 100+ list gets more challenging every year. There is just so much quality coming out at a furious rate. We still haven't come up with a better scientific system on how to construct this list. I put it together based on just a few things. First, this is the boom bap review. So, I look for albums with that boom and that bap: the thumping kick drum accented with a nice crisp snare. Second, I look for lyrics that go with the drums. Bonus points go towards lyricists providing thought-provoking or uplifting lyrics. For the top 30 I usually look for albums that are over 20 minutes in length. All albums in the book came out between November 6, 2021 and November 4th, 2022. That's about it, but not all of it.

I listen to the input of my crew of course. I also observe what people are talking about online. I follow Ian Charles of HHDG Media, Brutus Maximus and Raw Side Hip-Hop, Anthony L'Italien from Hip-Hop Lifers, Roger Folklorico, Ismail Ghedamsi-filio, and others. I see what they are listening to and read their commentary and observe how people respond. All of this plays a supporting role.

Again, this is not scientific. At the end of the day I pretty much make the final decision. What I try really, really hard to do is let the music guide me. I am but one person: one who has listened to boom bap Hip-Hop for decades with a particular affinity for the Native Tongues and any artist or group resembling that vibe. Still, just one person. Obviously, no one person can be the arbiter of what is or isn't dope. The main goal of this book has and will always be to preserve and advance Hip-Hop music. My hope is that you find an album that maybe you never heard before or stumble upon an artist that's new to you. You give it a shot and love it or at least appreciate it. My other hope is that you find any number of albums on this list and go buy them from the artist's Bandcamp. Let's support these incredible artists making our lives a little better by sharing some of their art. Here's to another great year and another painstakingly hard list to put together. We hope you enjoy it.

# CHAPTER ONE: THE TOP 30

# # 1

## *Cheat Codes*
## Black Thought & Danger Mouse

According to me (and the article I did in the *2020 Boom Bap Review*) Black Thought is the greatest of all time. Well, that's what I (MC Till) think at least. So might I be biased in putting his new album in the #1 slot? Perhaps. I could have gone with another legend, Nas and his album, *Magic*. I could have also gone with Muldrow and Elzhi as they made a funky boom bap lyrical masterpiece. It could have gone to one of the hardest working and most consistent emcees, The Bad Seed and his phenomenal *Four Ringer Ring*. Ghettosocks made a deserving album with DK. Tab-One made an incredible album worthy of the # 1 spot, too. But, the #1 can only go to one. I think Black Thought and

Danger Mouse stand out from the rest of the albums mentioned here even if ever so slightly. *Cheat Codes* to me has a certain expanding quality that gives me a little more with each listen. Another lyric to explore. A new sound I didn't hear quite the same way before. The album grows and gets better as it attaches itself to the listener. It is hard to explain but I definitely feel it and that unexplainable "it" propels the album to inch out all the other #1 spot contenders.

# #2

## *Zhigeist*
## Elzhi & Georgia Anne Muldrow

Elzhi has always been a spectacular emcee. Georgia Anne Muldrow has always been a brilliant creative emcee/producer who has a knack of blending boom bap, soul, and funk. That's exactly what she does for Elzhi. She winds up those funky boom bap pitches and Elzhi knocks them out of the park. The album sounds amazing and looks amazing too. One of a kind artist Dan Lish does the album cover design and it matches the quality of the music. Be amazed by the lyrical dexterity, the funky boom bap, and the visual images of *Zhigeist*.

## #3

## *Glory in the Weight*
## Tab-One

Wow. This album is sooo good. Tab-One has made good music before as a solo artist and as a member of Kooley High. But, I think this is his best work yet. The music is jazzy and soulful. The instrumentation is near perfect as Tab-One delivers an A+ performance. He is the master of each song. He is in control while simultaneously in service to the music. His vocals and creative style blends with the percussion so well. This album is like when I listen to an old jazz record and find that one loop where the horns, bass and drums all work together perfectly. That's this entire album. Glory be.

# # 4

## *Four Finger Ring*
## The Bad Seed

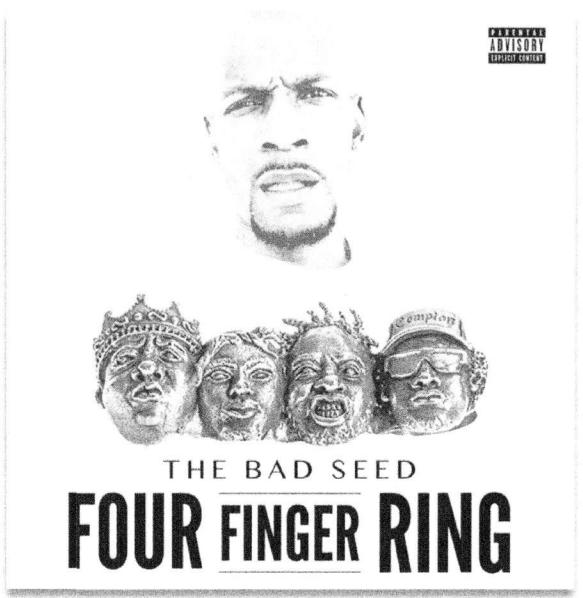

The Bad Seed has been making consistently good to great albums for the past several years. You can't find a bad album from him and he has a lot of albums lately to choose from. They're all good, but *Four Finger Ring* is the best to my ears. He gives us reflection, storytelling, and as always plenty of hard rhymes. And he does all of this over some of his best production yet. Which is an amazing thing to say because he always picks great beats. But, somehow, he found even better production for this release. Adding what I would call his best album to an already stellar catalog is pretty impressive.

## #5

## *Listen to the Masters*
## Ghettosocks and DK

DK is a dope producer who outdid himself with *Listen to the Masters*. His production throughout the album is vintage east coast boom bap that sounds as fresh as ever. Together with Ghettosocks they enlist an incredible supporting cast of masters including Skyzoo, Rome Streetz, O.C, CL Smooth, El Da Sensei and many others. Then there is Ghettosocks who has a great voice, thoughtful content, and an inviting presence on the mic. Great album!

# # 6

## *Magic*

## Nas

Nas has done it again. He teamed up with Hit-Boy and gave us a nine song no-skip project. Remember the last time Nas did that? Well, this time around is not going to live up to his debut, but it definitely doesn't disappoint either. Nas sounds inspired and hungry over noteworthy boom bap production. If this is Nas's victory lap, his strut sounds amazingly new and fresh. Nearly three decades later and Nas is still ill.

# # 7

## *Words to the Wise*
## Vic Monroe & Tone Spliff

Vic Monroe is like the wisdom of all the sage rappers before him, coupled with a voice that was gifted to him from B-Real and Guru (Rest in Peace). When Vic rhymes, you want to listen and take heed. It is easy to do so because his voice sounds so slick. It is authoritative, original, and unifying. All he needs are some dope beats and he is set. Thankfully Tone Spliff has that covered. His beats are exactly what is needed. His straight-forward *Low-End Theory* style bass, drums, and light sampling is the perfect fit for Vic's voice. Words to the wise over dope beats makes for a great listen.

# # 8

## *Infinite Wisdom*
## Awon & SOUL.DOPE.95

Awon is the definition of quality Hip-Hop. He never disappoints. Here on *Infinite Wisdom* he ventures out a bit from his usual sound. There are definitely plenty of moments that fit what one would expect from a new Awon album: jazzy horns, soulful beats, reflective lyrics presented in a straightforward laid-back way. But there are also moments of experiment: choppy-stuttering beats, a few drum sounds you might expect on a trap album, and lyrics delivered in double time. But don't let the experiment fool you. This album is rooted in a soulful sound that gives Awon some leverage to try out a few new things. And it all works!

# # 9

## *Sheep Stu*
## Dres & Stu Bangas

Normally an EP the length of *Sheep Stu* would not make the top 30. But like the essence of Hip-Hop we try hard not to box ourselves into arbitrary rules. When a project this dope falls short of the length we require for our top 30 well then we just have to break the rule. Rightfully so too. *Sheep Stu* features Dres, an emcee who stepped on the scene over 3 decades ago, sounding better than ever. He sounds hungry and Stu Bangas delivers the hard boom bap production to catapult this album into our top 10. Hope there is a sequel.

# # 10

## *Acres of Diamonds*
## ILL Conscious & Mute Won

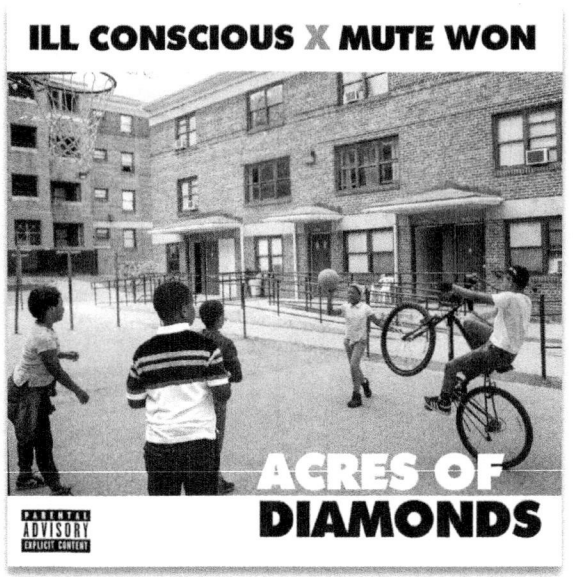

This man ILL Conscious can do no wrong. Every time he releases a project you know it is going to be quality. You are going to get one of the best lyrical deliveries in the game, thoughtful content, and soulful, raw boom bap production. That's exactly what ILL Conscious and Mute Won put together with *Acres of Diamonds*. This album also features some dope guests including Rome Streetz, Planet Asia, King Magnetik and many more. This is 15 tracks of great music.

# # 11

## *Harbor Kidz*
## Jamil Honesty & Squeegie Oblong

Jamil Honesty and Squeegie O are Harbor Kidz and it sounds amazing. It is rugged, underground Hip-Hop at its finest. Their energy is contagious. This album gives me early Wu-Tang Clan vibes. Their delivery is powerful and in-your-face. There is no getting away. The beats hold a similar element. The basslines grab you, introduce you to the drums and samples and the only thing you can do is nod your head. So stretch that neck and get ready.

# # 12

## *Smoking Gun*
## Deca

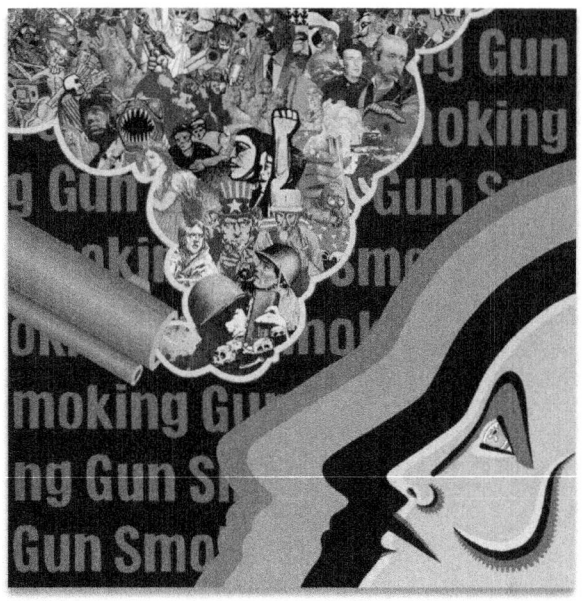

I am a huge fan of breakbeats and stand-up bass. So I love *Smoking Gun* because it is full of both. On top of those two elements, we also get jazzy samples and the serious voice and content from Deca. The thing about Deca's music is that his lyrical content is dense but the beats are not. The beats are lighter, playful at times. This juxtaposition of fun beats and serious rhymes works really well. You can just hit play and enjoy the music or sit down and be challenged by the lyrics or both.

# # 13

## *Deathfame*
## Quelle Chris

Quelle Chris remains a Hip-Hop heavyweight in a class of his own. His intoxicating originality is on full display throughout *Deathfame*. The album features a lot of drums and bass that have a pretty low-sounding frequency. This sounds great with Quelle's unique voice. Mix that winning combination along with really interesting lyrics and you have another great Quelle Chris album (and there are plenty). One more thing and I've said this before - Quelle Chris comes through again with some of the best basslines reminiscent of those thick, crunchy Eric Sermon-like basslines. So dope.

# # 14

## *Gold*
## Rigz & DJ Muggs

Rigz has an urgency in his voice that is only paralleled by a select few. It is almost like he doesn't have much time left and we don't know if he'll even get out the next lyric. It is that serious. So are the beats by Muggs. If you are not a fan of the drum-less production, then I think you'll really like the majority of this album. Muggs, with a few exceptions, brings loud, booming drums. I love it and this might just be my favorite Muggs production in recent years. It is that dope.

# # 15

## *The Elephant Man's Bones*
## Roc Marciano & The Alchemist

In my humble opinion this is Roc Marciano's best album since *Reloaded*. That's saying a lot because since then he has released nine albums, all of them good. But, The Alchemist pushes this one towards the top of his catalog. Yes, there are a few drum-less beats on here. But there are also plenty of hard-hitting drums and they are ever so soft, crisp, yet raw. The musical landscape is beautiful as Roc Marciano caresses the mic as only he can do.

# # 16

## *Church / Aethiopes*
## Billy Woods

Billy Woods brings something special with two albums this year - *Aethiopes* with production by Preservation and *Church* with beats by Messiah Musik. Both albums feature Billy Woods spitting words that demand a third and fourth and fifth listen. Okay, maybe a lifetime of re-listens! His dense lyrics are propelled by an unorthodox delivery that hangs in the pocket at times and at times rips it apart. *Aethiopes* has a bit smoother production with a more minimal percussive approach although the drums are definitely there. *Church* has more drums present but feels sparse since much of the album is slower than your typical boom bap Hip-Hop. Either way, Billy Woods shines on albums that we can go back to again and again and again and it never ends.

# #17

## *The Overview Effect*
## Jermiside & The Expert

What in the world is going on? Jermiside tackles the state of this messed up world over interesting, extraterrestrial beats from The Expert. The production feels traditional boom bap at times but also features minimal drums here and there. Regardless, the samples used are an interesting range. Interesting is a good word for this album. (I mean I've said three times now!) It can be enjoyed at first listen but the real magic of this album is the layered depth both in the production and Jermiside's lyrics. Put it on once and then again and again for maximum enjoyment.

# # 18

## *The W.O.W. (The Weight of Wind)*
## Cashus King

In an interview we did with Cashus King he revealed that this album was recorded several years back. Hard to believe because of how timely and fresh this album sounds. The production has a particular feel giving off some Native Tongues / Dilla vibes while Cashus King is doing nothing but ripping rapid fire lyrics throughout. It is an enjoyable album upon a first listen and grows stronger as you peel back each lyrical layer. Hopefully, Cashus King has more albums yet to be released:)

## #19

## *Global Scope* – Pete Flux & Parental
## *Down the Rabbit Hole* – Mattic & Parental

I paired these together because they have a very similar sound. Producer Parental is great on both. The beats are reminiscent of a very straightforward mid-'90s boom bap sound. However, they don't come across stale and dated but instead sound fresh and invigorating. Mattic and Pete Flux also channel a similar mid-'90s feel. Pete Flux can sometimes exhibit a slight pause and go element to his flow while Mattic gives us more of a smooth delivery. Both deliveries work really well over Parental's production for two stellar albums!

## #20

## *Food for Thought / The Last Remnants*
## Che Noir

You know how people in the world of entertainment or sports talk about a young talent that has "it?" You can't necessarily pinpoint *it* but you know that person has *it*. That's Che Noir to me. She just has *it*. Every time she spits a verse I want to listen. And listen I did! Che Noir gave us plenty to appreciate in 2022. She is excellent throughout both *Food for Thought* and *The Last Remnants* with her confident flow and the clever way she tugs at your emotions. She brings you in, sits you down, and serves you plate after plate. Listen. Think about it. The music tastes good.

# # 21

## *Set Out in the Dark*
## Mighty Theodore

Mighty Theodore comes through with perhaps the most chilled album of the century. From his laid-back singing to his low baritone rap voice to the lush soul samples over drums that never do too much, but just enough this album is pure drive-to music. I don't even have anywhere to go and I want to drive around town, slow, listening to this album with the volume all the way up. Mighty Theodore does an excellent job capturing a smooth atmosphere from the beginning to the end and features a host of all-star guests including Fly Anakin, SonnyJim, J Scienide, Hassaan Mackey, and many more. Job very well done!

## #22

## *The Art of Tradition*
## Kastaway & Cam the Downrocka

This album is a piece of underground, boom bap brilliance. Hailing from Chicago, IL, Kastaway has a classic Hip-Hop flow that packs a punch without being too wordy. The hard, soulful beats from Cam the Downrocka are the perfect musical landscape for Kastaway. If you grew up loving early '90s Hip-Hop, I think you will love this album. And regardless of when you grew up, if you like good music, I think you too will enjoy this album. It is pure Hip-Hop through and through and I love it.

# # 23

## *Marlowe 3*
## L'Orange & Solemn Brigham

These guys, L'Orange & Solemn Brigham, can do no wrong. They gave us their first album in 2018. It was so dope. They continued that dopeness in 2020 with *Marlowe 2* and now we must have been doing something right for these Hip-Hop gods to bless us with *Marlowe 3*. It is as good as, if not better than, their first two projects. Solemn Brigham continues to show why he is one of the best emcees out right now, showcasing different deliveries as he rides over L'Orange's production like a pro. And L'Orange's beats range from in-the-pocket L'Orange sounding beats (dope) to slightly experimenting with a few new sample sounds and new drum sounds (also dope). These guys are pure dope every time. Press play and enjoy!

# # 24

## *The Sundown EP*
## Freddie Marr & Th.iii.rd

If you are a Hip-Hop head outside of Buffalo, that city's name might make you think about Griselda. But I want you to forever think about Freddie Marr & the Th.iii.rd from here on out. They made an incredible, soulful, Native Tongues-esque project in *The Sundown EP*. Th.iii.rd is that guy in class that never seems to study but aces every test. His subtle skills bring you into his world and it sounds lovely. Freddie Marr's beats are equally fresh. This is a match made in Heaven, well, Buffalo. What did you just think about? (It better have been Freddie Marr & Th.iii.rd!!!)

# # 25

## *To Dream in Color*
## Rapper Big Pooh

Big Pooh takes a page right out of his Little Brother cohort Phonte's playbook, and delivers a boom bap project sprinkled with plenty of R&B soul. This is a very mature album with Big Pooh opening up and sharing about interpersonal relationships, mental health issues, and more. He does all of this over production that makes even the most serious of subjects go down easy. It is at times lush with strings and synths ("Changing Again") and other times a bit more rough but still smooth ("1 Day in NY"). Either way it is a quality album that gives the listener great insights into Pooh's life combined with really great production.

# # 26

## *Chosen*
## Eddie Kaine & K Sluggah

This is my sleeper album of the year album. Eddie Kaine has a ravaging hunger in his voice. It is intense. It is commanding. He just goes after it in a straightforward way but every once in a while he catches a fun wave on top of the beat and flexes some stylistic changes to keep things interesting. The beats that K Sluggah provides are some of my favorites of the year; from the energy of "Warm it Up" to the somber feel of "No Smoke", to my absolute favorite which is the title track "Chosen." Don't sleep.

# # 27

## *Eat the Kiwi Skin*
## Isatta Sheriff & Koralle

London, UK emcee Isatta Sheriff knows how to rhyme and how to put a project together. *Eat the Kiwi Skin* is a beautiful blend of positive flows over jazzy boom bap production. Producer Koralle brings forth pianos and horns with head-snapping drum patterns while Isatta shines through spitting bars and singing a bit. She can do no wrong. So, grab that kiwi, rub it down with a towel, eat the entire thing and turn this album all the way up!

# # 28

## *Martian XMAS 2021*
## Moka Only

If you locked yourself in a dungeon and listened to *Fan-tas-tic Vol. 1* by Slum Village and then tried to recreate that sound, you would get *Martian XMAS 2021* by Moka Only. Being that *Fantastic Vol. 1 and 2* are two of my favorite albums in the world, I love this vibe from Moka Only. Every song has a similar feel with deep, head nodding kick drums, loud crackling snares, and vintage basslines with sparse sampling complimenting it all. Beautiful.

# # 29

## *Between Us and the World EP. 1: Amped Up /*
## *Between Us and the World EP 2: The Good Shepard*
## Act Proof

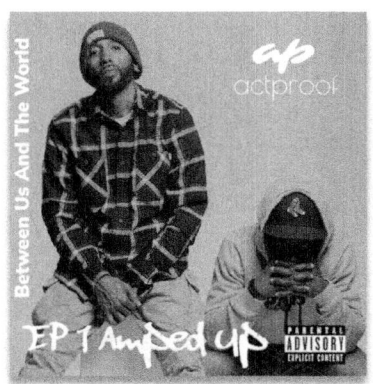 

Two emcees, Enigma and Sundown, are Act Proof. No gimmicks. Just pure music. These two EPs make for a great listen. They are filled with expert rhyming and fantastic production. Both EPs have a very nostalgic feel to them while remaining new and fresh. There must be something in the water in Raleigh, NC because the Hip-Hop coming out of that city seems to be superior in every way. Act Proof is no exception. Need proof? Just listen to these two fantastic EPs and you'll have all the proof you need, although you will definitely want more.

# # 30

*The World Changed* – **Napoleon Da Legend & Amerigo Gazaway**
*Modus Operandi* – **Napoleon Da Legend & Just Music Beats**
*Versatilis Prolificus* – **Napoleon Da Legend & Gyver HYPMAN**
*Maison de Medici* – **Napoleon Da Legend & Clypto**
*The Colossus of GOATS* – **Napoleon Da Legend**

Over the past few years, I've listened to so many Napoleon Da Legend albums and they are all quality. How does this man put out so many solid albums? This is no easy task but somehow he has done it and continues to do it. And this is perplexing to me. Instead of trying to figure out which Napoleon album is the best, I decided to list all the albums he put out this year and give each one an award.

Most Innovative goes to *Two Piece*
MC Till's personal favorite: *Versatilis Prolificus*
The Most Chill Album Award: *Maison de Medici*
The Don't Forget About this Album 'cause it too is Dope goes to *Modus Operandi*
The Straightforward Boom Bap Bliss album: *The World Changed*
The "Oh wait, he released yet another album" award goes to *The Colossus of GOATS*

## CHAPTER TWO: ALBUMS 31 – 50

### 31
### *Omowale*
### Wildchild

### 32
### *The List God Sent Us*
### OC from NC

### *33*
### *Projext Pyrvmids*
### Sonny Paradise

34
*Never at Peace*
**Career Crooks**

35
*1993 / ONYX vs Everybody*
**ONYX**

36
*The Forever Story*
**JID**

37

*Life is More than White Bricks*

**WateRR & Vanderslice**

38

*Black Vladimir*

**Meyhem Lauren**

39

*Secret Wars*

**Raz Fresco & Dibia$E**

40
## *Czarmageddon!*
### Czarface

41
## *The Don & Eye*
### The Musalini & 9th Wonder

42
## *Up Against the Wall; A Degree of Lunacy*
### YUNGMORPHEUS & Theravada

## 43
## *GOD CMPLX*
### Sol Messiah

## 44
## *Deutsche Marks 3*
### Willie the Kid & V Don

## 45
## *Mudslide*
### Vic Spencer & Small Professor

46
## *Bring Me Back When the World Is Cured*
### Kno & Sadistik

47
## *Forever*
### Phife Dawg

48
## *2000*
### Joey Bada$$

49
*Raw Extractions*
Lukah

50
*Don't Wait For Me to Leave*
Zilla Rocca & andrew

# CHAPTER THREE: ALBUMS 51 – 100+

51
### *Heist the Crown*
### Planet Asia & Body Bag Ben

52
### *In the Beginning Vol. 2*
### Declaime & Madlib

53
### *The In and Out of Love Tape*
### Funky DL

54
## *Back in Black*
### Cypress Hill

55
## *a tape called component system with the auto reverse*
### Open Mike Eagle

56
## *Hell's Road*
### Hell Razah

57
## *Live from the End of the World, Vol. 1 (Demos)*
### Blu & Fatlip

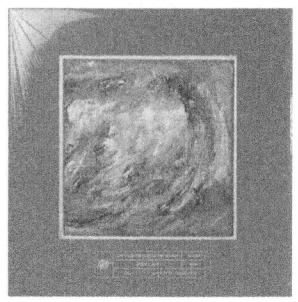

58
## *Meth Lab Season 3: The Rehab*
### Method Man

59
## *For the FKN Love*
### Arrested Development

60
## *Black Light*
### Stalley & Apollo Brown

61
## *Bonafide*
### MC Melodee & Cookin Soul

62
## *Dad's House*
### Starvin B

63
*Murder Castle*
**IAMGAWD**

64
*Three*
**Justo the MC & maticulous**

65
*No Fear of Time*
**Black Star**

66
## *Vinyl Days*
Logic

67
## *Eat*
Pan Amsterdam & Damu the Fudgemunk

68
## *Frank*
Fly Anakin

### 69
## *Metatron's Cube* – AJ Suede & Televangel
## *Oil on Canvas* – AJ Suede

### 70
## *Americancer*
### Paten Locke

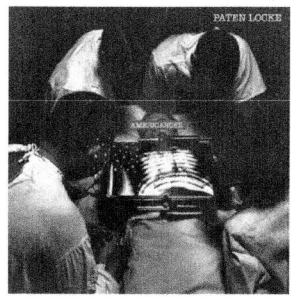

### 71
## *The North Star: Love of the Art*
### Brandon Isaac & Free Mind

## 72
## *The Fragility of Life*
**Wordsworth**

## 73
## *You Want a Piece of Me?*
**Es**

## 74
## *Here Goes Nothing*
**Shortie No Mass**

75
## *Wolves Don't Eat with Shepherd's*
### Knowledge the Pirate

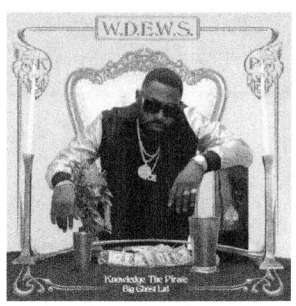

76
## *Killing Nothing*
### Boldy James and Real Bad Man

77
## *Stone Cold Killer*
### Zagnif Nori

78

*The Monolithic Era* – SUBSTANCE810 & JQuest Beatz
*Desolate Lands* – SUBSTANCE810

79

*The Pantheon*
Body Bag Ben & JR Swiftz

80

*Rx*
Rasheed Chappell & Xp The Marxman

81
## *Remedy Meets Wu-Tang*
**Remedy**

82
## *God Don't Make Mistakes /*
## *What Has Been Blessed Cannot Be Cursed*
**Conway the Machine**

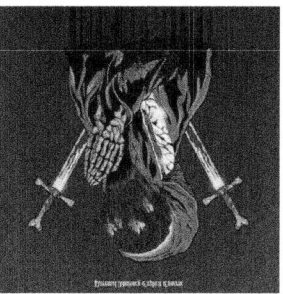

83
## *Reclamation*
**BambuDeAsiatic**

84
## *Tana Talk 4*
### Benny the Butcher

85
## *2econd Cousins*
### 5ifth Element & Dee Jackson

86
## *Writer Fluid*
### Cas Metah

87
*Smooth Boxcutta*
The Benchwarmers Clique

88
*Course of the Inevitable 2*
Lloyd Banks

89
*Dimensions of Dialogue*
Penpals

90
*The People's Champ*
Dell-P

91
*My Life Iz a Movie*
RJ Payne

92
*KOTODAMA*
1773 & EBrown

93

## *The R.A.W. EP / The Queen's Gambit / Californication*
**YaH-Ra**

94

## *Yodney Dangerfield / Yod Stewart*
**Your Old Droog**

95

## *Book of Changes*
**Noveliss & Dixon Hill**

96
## *Random Thoughts*
### Thought Provokah

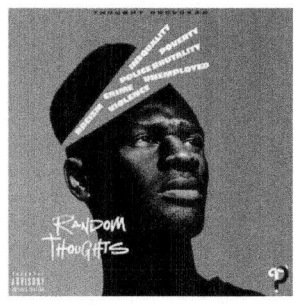

97
## *Mountain God*
### Poe Mack

98
## *For all Intents and Purposes*
### Truth & Da Beatminerz

99
## *Joyland*
### Stik Figa & Conductor Williams

100
## *Wreckage Manner*
### Havoc & Styles P

101
## *Third Stone*
### Greg Cypher & Def Dee

102
## *Golden Era: Timeless*
### L'undercover & Mic Handz

## Honorable Mentions

*From the Slumz* - Benny Slumz & Tone Spliff
*Giant in the Mental* - A.G.
*Figure 8 / Lost in the Wilderness / She Loves Me, She Loves Me Not / The Birds, The Bees And Everything in Between* - Cashus King
*Jazz* - Fredro Starr
*These Never Dropped* - Adagio!
*Change Ya Views* - Scienz of Life
*Space Bar* - Your Old Droog
*Chaotic Good* - Patterns of Chaos
*Surface Noise* - Lars Viola
*Shadow Self* - Sleep Sinatra, Ohbliv
*Subterranean Obscura* - Reckonize Real
*DRUG-Politix 2: GAWD Has No Face* - Precyce Politix & D.R.U.G.S. Beats
*Project Near You* - SmooVth
*It's Almost Dry* - Pusha T
*Mother in Peace* - 2033 & Venomous2000 & Chinch 33
*Then Again* - The Primitive One
*Guttersnipe* - Saga
*Continuance* - Curren$y & The Alchemist
*3rd Chamber Grail Bars* - Cappadonna & Stu Bangas
*Exquisite Villainry* - New Villain
*Stranded in Foggy Times* - Verb T & Ill Informed
*Somebody's Paradise / Kaput* - J Scienide
*The Ceremony of Innocence* - Krohme
*Mood Swings* - Smoke DZA & Real Bad Man
*Don't Make Me Famous* - NapsNdreds
*The Realness II* - Cormega
*Handz of Stone* - ethemadassassin

## Super Short EPs and Other Spectacular Things

*Seven Pt. III* - Awon, Seb Zillner, & A N T I T H E S I S
*An Evening with Silk Sonic* - Silk Sonic
*The Three Fantastic Supermen Epics* - Killah Priest
*Guilty by Association* - Guilty Simpson & Phro
*Black Be the Source* - Fly Anakin, Pink Siifu, & Billz Egypt
*Weather Report Two EP* - J.Arrr x K!ng Jvmes
*Language Arts* - Ka
*Woeful Studies* - Ka
*Neo Griot & The Afrocentric Prince* - Neo Griot & The Afrocentric Prince
*Tongue Fu* - Nejma Nefertiti
*Mural of Rhymes* - S Eyes Finest

## Albums We Missed in 2020

*The Rufus Buck Project* - Jamil Honesty
*Truth is Underrated* - Emskee & MiLKCRATE

# Part Two
# LONG-FORM REVIEWS

# CHAPTER FOUR
## *Glory in the Weight*
### Tab-One
#### Written by MC Till

Sometimes an album comes out of nowhere to surprise me. I don't know the caliber of the emcee and have relatively no expectations going in and it just blows me away. *The Element of Surprise* by Rashad and Confidence is such an album. If you haven't heard of it, I suggest you visit Google. Other times an emcee is known for their quality and releases an album that far surpassed my expectations. OC did this with *Jewelz*. Sure, OC was incredible. His debut was incredible. But *Jewelz* took it to another level. I wasn't surprised that it was good. I was surprised that it was way better than good. And this is the case with *Glory in the Weight* by Tab-One.

Tab-One is no slouch when it comes to dope music. He has been around for a long time propelling good music and the culture forward. He did this in college by organizing Hip-Hop events. He did this as part of Inflowential, as a part of Kooley High, and he has also done it as a solo emcee releasing a few really dope projects. His last album, *Balancing Act,* came out in 2020 and was excellent. So I headed into his new album knowing that it would be good. But oh my goodness, I didn't realize it would be this good!

The very first song "Keep On" perfectly sets the mood for the rest of the album which is a comfortable experience. The bass throughout the album offers a nice landing pad for the listener to get situated. Tab-One's presence is a gift. He has something to say. He has plenty to say actually as he opens up throughout the album. However, it is his delivery that makes all his content go down so easily. His voice is not disrupting. It settles into the production and becomes another instrument. "Keep On" does all of this right away so we know what we just stepped into.

It only gets better. In fact, two of my favorite songs on the album are the last two! This album is like the gift that keeps on giving! More on those two later. First I want to highlight something else I absolutely love on this album. We can hear it as soon as track #3 "Do Work" comes on: keys. But not like traditional piano keys. These are like Fender Rhodes keys and they are so beautiful. That sound doesn't stop after "Do Work." Nope. It is just getting started. We hear this similar instrument throughout the album. Again, just so beautiful.

Then there are the drums. Some are really getting into that minimal drum movement and that's cool. I like some of it, especially KA who I think is one of the greatest emcees ever. Period. But, I like drums! And the drums on this album are great. They fit the vibe so, so well. Nothing feels out of place. There are conga sounds, great usage of high hats, deep kicks, soulful crispy snares and rim shots: it is all there. Every song features the coming together of every instrument along with Tab-One's voice to create a darn near perfect feel. Did I say this was a really good album?

Finally, let me suggest that Tab-One is masterful in his lyrical delivery. I already mentioned that he does a great job of making his voice sound like another instrument. In addition, he shares some very heartfelt lyrics that connect. He does this throughout the album but I want to dive into the final two songs to illustrate this point. On "Self Doubt" he raps, *Doomed by ego and vacuums of vanity. Don't let it suck you in. Go and handle it. I dove into doubt and then emerged with a candle lit and I'm sick of job interviews asking about my passion. It ain't that I ain't got it. It's just that I got to ration it.* That very last line does a few things. First, it provides a glimpse and offers an invitation. Well, why does Tab-One have to ration his passion? Do I have to do that? Why can't I give myself fully to my passion? You see what's happening. This line provides for a dialogue with the listener. The other thing it does is showcase how a line on paper can be good but when you hear it, it is so much better! I mean that's a dope line. It has meaning. It's cool. But when you hear how he delivers it you experience how beautiful words can sound when rapped rhythmically over the perfect beat. Give it a listen and see if you agree.

The final song on the album is probably my favorite, "Breath." I love everything about this song. The lyrical content, the beat, the hook, the verses, everything. It just makes me want to be happy. After an album full of melancholy reflection, this is the perfect ending. It is more upbeat in tone, more hopeful. Just breathe. It is going to be okay. *Just remember to breathe. Thought I heard God whispering in the breeze. As it moved through the leaves in the trees. Felt a calm wash over. Walked in the ease.*

There you go. Regardless of whether you believe in God or divinity, I think we can agree that there is beauty in this world. I definitely found it while listening to *Glory in the Weight*. I do every time I give it another spin. Now, let's see if you do too.

## CHAPTER FIVE
### *Four Finger Ring*
### The Bad Seed
#### Written by MC Till

*Four Finger Ring* is the hardest boom bap album of the year. No doubt about it in my mind. In some ways The Bad Seed is like the Roc Marciano of hard boom bap production. Or you could say Roc Marci is the laid back, drumless version of The Bad Seed. But the comparison is helpful in that both emcees have been making incredible music in recent years. One (Roc) went the less-drums-is-more approach while The Bad Seed went all in for hard drums and thumping basslines and it worked. And while Roc Marci has that more vulnerable voice that kind of creeps and meanders over the eerie production, The Bad Seed's powering presence fits perfectly with the stellar boom bap production. His voice is deep, paralleling the pitch of the Rockness Monster from the Boot Camp Clik. It rattles the soul. It doesn't invite you into the music, it stretches out its arm, grabs the listener by the throat, and demands attention. One has no choice.

And this new album, *Four Finger Ring*, is as good as it gets. He has outdone himself once again. It is every bit as hard as previous releases. Yet, there are also moments of solace. Even though the majority of the album tends to live on the more violent, hardcore, in-your-face side of the mountain, I want to tune into the other side. Or at least the moments that point to another side. Being that I'm a huge Native Tongues fan and gravitate to that kind of style both in content and musically, I love when harder artists reflect on more emotionally universal themes. So, let's explore that.

We will start with the semi-confessional track *Just Be True*. Not confessional in the traditional sense but The Bad Seed is reaching out to so-called fans wondering where the support is; *Send messages to fans but none of them write back* and *They love you now, but they don't show you. Fire emoji is not enough, bandcamp, buy the stuff.* On this second song from the album he promises to bring the fire and is rightfully convinced that his music is dope enough for any Hip-Hop fan's support. Yet, he wonders where it is! So to me it is like a confession where he is admitting that he does not get the love he should. It's like he is saying, "Look, I'm here. I've been here. I've been dope. What's going on? Why don't I get more support?" I find that very relatable. How often do we strive to be great at home with our kid(s) or with a partner, at work or school, or wherever? We constantly try and try only to feel like it goes unnoticed or under appreciated. The Bad Seed is describing this space and many of us can feel that kind of frustration. He does a great job wrapping up that emotion into the song.

A few songs later he gives us the chilling track, "Bloody Rain" where he states *Bloody rain falling on the city. God Crying.* He goes on to rap about school shootings and the apathy that assists them, *They shootin' schools up. (The) system ain't given' 2 f\*cks... Imagine bein' 9 going to school. Cool stuff. Somebody come in shooting, killin people that you trust. Friends, teachers, janitors. Everybody, the news truck outside. Sirens blarin. You scared. You stuck. Hidin' under tables in class, hopin the dude runs out of all his amo. Gotta wait until the blue comes. God shed a few tears with me.* Then it is back into that refrain of *Bloody rain falling on the city. God Crying.* The image of God's tears falling on us in the form of blood is a chilling reality of the violence that plagues so many with growing indifference from so many more. I used to live in a neighborhood riddled with violence. I wrote some songs about that very community in a way that highlighted the violence while seeming detached from it. I remember a mentor of mine at the time challenged me to enter into the story: to write empathetically by taking the lament approach. This is what the Bad Seed has done. He is not removed from the violence. He is not judging the people being torn apart by it. He is in it expressing the agony. It is one of the highest forms of art imo and extremely compelling.

The final song I want to highlight and celebrate is "Think About You." This song is a dedication to folks near and dear to The Bad Seed that have passed away into another form. Maybe these fallen brothers and sisters can hear this beautiful song. If so they'll hear the hook, *Even though you not here, I still think about you. The World is what I think about you. And I'mma still move the earth without fear but I'm sick without you.* What beautiful words that the masses can relate to. I know I can as I've lost some pretty close people to death. Still, and in their honor, I must move without fear like The Bad Seed mentions in the hook. In part, I must live my life to the fullest to honor those who are not here. I think we must all find a way forward that is fulfilling even while we mourn loss.

Likewise, in the midst of violence we must find moments of vulnerability and honesty ("Just be True") and reflective moments to lament for others ("Bloody Rain") along with the courage to live life to the fullest while remembering those who are no longer with us ("Think About You"). The Bad Seed gives us glimpses of hope and inspiration throughout an album that is otherwise filled with harsh realities of life. This is true on the very last song on the album where The Bad Seed gives us an opportunity to reimagine a violent tool, the four finger ring. On the cover of the album, the four finger ring enshrines four fallen Hip-Hop greats; Biggie, 2Pac, Ol' Dirty Bastard, and Eazy-E.

Two of these artists died from poor choices and perhaps bad luck. The other two died violent deaths, both were gunned down in horrific fashion. One of the last things The Bad Seed says on this album is *Protect your energy, baby. The Four Finger Ring… Let's get into this f\*\*\*in album.* Earlier in that song he emphasizes that the four finger ring can be used as a tool to navigate a violent Hip-Hop high school. Hip-Hip is all about metaphors. Or at least metaphors are used frequently in Hip-Hop music. Some might listen to this album and hear the gunshots in the background and the aggressive imagery and think the album is promoting violence. I hear something else… I hear someone relating to that world. He is speaking the language of a world that is not nice and neat and cozy and safe, but not staying in that world totally. In fact he's living in it, describing it and sprinkling in beautiful foreshadowing of what could be.

It is easy to judge. And judging someone's art can bring quick bursts of satisfaction. But it is a shallow and fleeting feeling. To sit with someone's art that might disagree with your perspective or expectations is more challenging. Yet it yields a much more meaningful result. It can bring understanding and empathy which can go a long way. I assume this is part of The Bad Seed's secret. I think he relates to the very people he writes about in his music. He doesn't judge. He speaks a common language and does it over hard boom bap production. I for one appreciate it, enjoy it, and am challenged by it. So give it a listen and if nothing else, take heed to The Bad's Seed parting advice… *protect your energy baby.*

# CHAPTER SIX
## *Magic\**
## Nas

Written by MC Till

"Nas picks trash beats." You've probably heard that before. Sure, in the span of his nearly 30 years in Hip-Hop, has Nas picked some beats that I wasn't feeling? Yes. Is that abnormal for someone of his pedigree? Not really. What's abnormal is for an artist like Nas to be around this long, remain so relevant, and produce music that is still impactful. His 14th studio album, *Magic*, just might be his best work of art since *It Was Written*.

*Magic* packs all the necessary elements for me - dope lyrics, great delivery, and boom bap production. It is what both *Kings Disease* albums achieved in parts. On both *1* and *2* Nas and Hit-Boy made some pre-magic happen. They had moments that were incredible. However, they also had moments that just didn't seem to fit. That's not the case with *Magic*. Everything fits on this short 9 song album. I wonder if Nas and Hit-Boy had that infallible classic *Illmatic* in mind when they selected those 9 joints as that's the same amount of songs on that brilliant debut. Nine seems to be a lucky number for Nas.

Months before the release of *King's Disease I* by Nas and Hit-Boy, I predicted it would be his best album since *Illmatic*, even better than his sophomore album, *It Was Written*. Nas won his first grammy for *KD1*, but I don't think that album climbed up into Nas' top five best efforts, let alone rivaling *IWW*. However, Nas and Hit-Boy were on the right track. They remained on that path for *KD2* with a more sultry and cohesive boom bap experience. Still, there were songs on that project that seemed out of place.

Songs like "40 Side," "EPMD 2," and "YKTV" did not add to the synergy of the album and in my opinion detracted from it. But, on *Magic* I think they figured it out. They created a project that felt right and exact from the first song to the last. It is a shorter album, but it's more poignant and tighter.

Hit-Boy is able to create beats that are both head-nodders for the boom bap purist and easily digestible vibes for the casual music fan to enjoy. You hear it in the crisp drums and bass on "Speechless" and "Meet Joe Black." You definitely hear it in the fresh yet old school sounding beat for "Wave Gods." That's probably my favorite song on the album. It features the only guest emcee of the album, A$AP Rocky, who has such a great emcee voice. The two craft nostalgic verses over the throwback sounding beat that comes equipped with a scratched hook by the legend, DJ Premier. Plus they throw a nod to Gang Starr in the chorus. So much to love about this song!

May I remind you that *Illmatic* hit the scene in 1994. A few years before that, Nas spit his seminal verse on "Live at the Barbecue." That's over 30 years ago. Three decades is a long time. In Hip-Hop years that's like 300 years! It is difficult for many emcees of that era to spit with a similar hunger in their voice. Nas does it. Nas sounds as inspired and hungry as ever on every single verse here. Perhaps that's the reason for the album title. Or maybe the magic comes from Hit-Boy who is also sounding nice as ever on the production. Lyrically, Nas sounds like a veteran with youthful energy while Hit-Boy is the youthful energy with veteran poise. It all works well.

Back in June of 2022 when Boston was up 2-1 on Golden State in the NBA finals I heard some pundits blasting Steph Curry.

And how did Curry respond? With his 4th ring in 8 years putting on a 3 point shooting clinic and winning his first finals MVP of his career. I'm not sure if he heard the critics or not, but they certainly heard his response! Turning back to Nas and how I opened this review, I've heard plenty of Hip-Hop fans criticize him for his bad beat selection. Like Curry, Nas responds with a masterful and magical performance with *Magic* which one could argue is one of his best. Give it a listen and enjoy.

*Author's Note - KDIII by Nas came out after the submission date for this book, but best believe it will be listed in our next book:)

## CHAPTER SEVEN
*Sheep Stu*
Dres & Stu Bangas
Written by MC Till

Dres was just minding his business being the dope Native Tongues person that he is when someone tagged him in an Instagram post. The post was a beat by Stu Bangas with a question that went something like this, *Who would sound dope over this beat?* Someone thought Dres would and tagged him in a comment. Dres then listened to the beat and was impressed. He heard more beats from Stu Bangas and was further impressed. He liked how the beats had a hard feel to them yet had so much soul. He was convinced and what ensued led to the creation of five incredible songs in the form of the *Sheep Stu* EP.

This project is the coming together of a legendary emcee who has remained a skilled craftsman of his art for over 3 decades and a not-all-that-younger producer who has been underground cooking up aggressive, soulful beats. By underground I only mean a subset of listeners who really get into an independent and more "old school" aural aesthetic that is more about authentic art than commercial success. Although, it is good to keep in mind that music from the underground often creeps up to a wider audience. I think *Sheep Stu* has the opportunity to break through in this way: to rise from its underground, boom bap roots and grow up into a world inhabited by many, many more people. For Dres, who earned this kind of success on steroids in the '90s, this will not be a foreign experience. For Stu Bangas, on the other hand I think it will. I could be wrong about that and he might not care one way or another. But the thought that his beats will be introduced to a larger audience is really exciting to me. He is one of the best boom bap producers around and he doesn't seem like the type to change his style just to get likes, follows, or shares. Like Dres, his flag has been planted and if people want to come to him and appreciate his music, they can. If not, the flag remains.

And it is planted in some fertile soil. Stu Bangas is great, providing production for Esoteric, Ill Bill, Nowaah the Flood, Recognize Ali, Capadonna, and many more including most recently a project with RJ Payne. So a great and prolific emcee meets a stellar producer. The result is nothing but dope. Yes, this EP is short with just 5 songs. It features one guest emcee in A.G. of DITC. That's it. No gimmicks. Just great music.

Dres continues to display a top tier delivery. His ability to play around with the inflection of words is amazing. He holds syllables as sacred, offering each one its own attention. Stu Bangas does something similar with his sound. Nothing is out of place, from the booming drums to all the different sounds layered on top. Like what Dres appreciated from hearing that beat on Instagram, the true magic to Stu Bangas is his ability to create a soulful sound that is simultaneously hard and rugged.

It is hard to pick any one song to highlight because they are all so dope and because it is such a short project. However, if I had to pick one, it would have to be "Killin It (For a Little Bit)." This song is the perfect example of how Dres's lyrical style and Stu's production chops go so well together. The title track, "Sheep Stu" also exemplifies this perfect union. Who am I kidding, they all do! I think so at least. What about you? Have you heard it? If not, give it a listen, then let us know what you think!

# CHAPTER EIGHT
## *Acres of Diamonds*
### Ill Conscious & Mute Won
#### Written by MC Till

Few emcees have the quality output of Baltimore emcee, Ill Conscious. I was introduced to his work through his phenomenal 2018 album *The Prerequisite*. He followed that up in 2019 outdoing himself with *Logistix*. In 2020 he gave us *The Epic of Gilgamesh* and followed that EP up with another shorter album in *Import Export*. I continue to revisit each of these projects as they are worthy of infinite repeat listens. So, did Ill Conscious do it again in 2022? Resoundingly yes!

*Acres of Diamonds* features Ill Conscious on the mic and Mute Won on the beats; neither artist disappoints. Few, if any, of today's emcees are on Ill's level lyrically. His ability to twist words around each other and flow them effortlessly across the beats is second to none. While other emcees sometimes come across subdued or lacking excitement, Ill brings energy and lots of it. Furthermore, he has something to say. He is witnessing life and translating it to us. He is not glorifying the pitfalls of life but reporting them. He gives us listeners a way in that we might not otherwise have access to.

It is not all reporting. He also channels the emcee gods of the past and employs Black excellence, self-empowerment, and an overall inspirational message. One hint of this is on "Paragon" where he rhymes, *my passage is reenactment of the African folklore*. On the same song the hook features scratch vocals from a few legendary emcees including Rakim and Brother J from XCLAN. It is as if by tying in these emcees he is bringing to life that 'reenactment' to include not only himself but a lineage of black excellence. It is only right that after "Paragon" he then transitions to his song, "Lineage" where he pays homage to those that helped shape him and offers condolences for those not here. It is on this song where we get a great insight into how Ill Conscious sees himself, "Somewhere in between a drug dealer and a freedom fighter." This one line helps us see the complexity of a brilliant artist striving to be something great while simultaneously being rooted in the same soil that also provides the fertile ground for destruction and violence. He is clearly a leader, but one that leads from within and is part of the community vs one that tries to exalt himself onto a self-made, self-righteous pedestal.

It is this conflicted yet steady leadership that I think I appreciate the most from Ill Conscious. I absolutely love Hip-Hop music that has this element - striking a balance between positivity and being dope seems to be a missing art-form these days. So much music is littered with gun talk and aggression. I would make the case that this music is needed in some capacity because it reflects a reality for some. However, an emcee like Ill Conscious is able to beautifully dance that ever thinning line between being empowering and uplifting and being honest and real. He does it so well, perhaps better than anyone out right now.

He has great depth and meaning to his lyrics. Amazingly, how he delivers his words is as good as his content if not better. So what about his beats?! Thankfully his beat selection and who he chooses to work with for projects is top notch. I think his ear for beats rivals Skyzoo's who also has an impeccable ear for amazing production. This go around Ill Conscious teams up with Mute Won who provides top notch beats throughout this project. Quoting from the album's Bandcamp, "With Baltimore and

Camden being similar in its grungy aesthetic, the artistic chemistry between ILL & Mute will serve as promising to the listener." I couldn't agree more. This duo sounds flawless together. I love the breakbeat driven drums and light sampling leaving room for Ill's ill performance. It almost feels like Mute One and Ill Conscious tried to outdo each other and in so doing the listener won big time.

I'll leave you with one more quote from the album. On "Black Czars" featuring Rome Streetz & Planet Asia, Ill Conscious raps *they white washin this, but (I put) my faith in the black parts*. While some artists from every genre of music sell a little piece of their soul trying to achieve success, Ill Conscious is much more interested in being his authentic self. You get the sense that he wants to move forward whether we go with him or not. I say, let's go! I don't think he'll lead us astray.

# CHAPTER NINE
## *The Sundown E.P.*
### Th.iii.rd & Freddie Marr
#### Written by MC Till

Most boom bap heads know about Buffalo. How can we not? The Griselda crew is everywhere, even appearing on late night talk shows. However, there is another Hip-Hop movement in Buffalo that you might not know about. Before the world came to associate Griselda with Buffalo, a very different Hip-Hop scene was emerging. There is a really great interview in TheFindMag.com entitled *The Resourceful Illery of Pseudo Intellectuals* by Danny that I highly recommend. This interview speaks to the Buffalo scene and how the Pseudo Intellectuals came together. Buffo wasn't always just doot, doot, doots, and high end fashion. It still isn't.

Enter *The Sundown E.P.* by Th.iii.rd and Freddie Marr. This album popped up on my radar thanks to our good friend Ismail Ghedamsi-filion. He posted it on a FB group and I'm so thankful he did. I hit that link and about 20 minutes later I reached out to Th.iii.rd to invite him onto our podcast. I had to get to know this emcee. His EP with Freddie Marr is both on point lyrically and production wise. But that's not all. He is not just a good lyricist, he is an intellectual able to deliver poignant attacks at society's ills in a way that sounds fresh and heartfelt. This is a rare trait and he has it.

Oh, and it gets better. I have so many positive things to say about this project. Okay, so he is able to drive home a positive, uplifting point. He can also rhyme, like really well and in a subtle way. Go listen to his verse on "Figaro." My goodness. This guy is just chilling in his crib, hand wrapped around a peach Snapple, legs up on the ottoman, gaze slightly fixed on the warmth of the sun breaking through the window, while taking out every emcee you and I think is great. This dude is dope by his presence.

Okay, okay, so Th.iii.rd has something empowering to say and he can rhyme with the best of them. There is more. His voice is golden. He has that smooth, boom bap Hip-Hop voice of wisdom. It just sounds dope and smart. Regardless of what he says, it sounds like he should have said it and we should have listened. And it is easy to digest - silky smooth with just the right amount of grit. Like Kev Brown mixed with J. Cole. No, maybe Kev Brown mixed with Finale. I don't know. You just need to listen to him and tell me your mixture equation.

Okay, okay, okay so he has the message, the lyrical skills, the voice, and, you guessed it, there is more reverence. The fourth song on this short project is "Untitled (Fantastic)" with Nelson Rivera on saxophone. On this song he throws a nod to Slum Village and one of the greatest songs, albums, and beat smiths this world has ever known - "Untitled," *Fan-Tas-Tic Vol. 2,* and Jay Dilla. It gets better. The very next song is entitled "All Vibes" and features DJ Cutler cutting up the "vibes, vibrations" sample popularized by De La Soul on their smash single "Stakes is High." This guy and the production team are cut from a dope, Native Tongue cloth.

Okay, okay, okay, okay let me go ahead and say a word about that Native Tongue cloth and speak about the production. Freddie Marr is the production duo of Tone (of the Pseudo Intellectuals) and Tommy Quattro (of 25 Metro). I wish I could claim that I've known about this production duo for years, but that would be lying. I only know because it states it on the Bandcamp page for this album that I only discovered through Ismael. Anway, the beats! Oh, the beats. If you have followed me at all, you probably know I'm a huge Native Tongues head. A lot of my favorite emcees, albums, beats, etc… come from that collective. The beats on this album are 100% on some Native Tongues vibes. The two songs I mentioned in the previous paragraph are Native Tongues all the way and that is true of the rest of the project as well. So if you like those subtle, soulful samples mixed with break beat driven drums, then you will appreciate the musicianship of this album.

In closing, I'd like to just apologize for using so many okays. And I'd also like to claim the obvious, I love this album. My only frustration is its length. With just 6 songs and a little under 20 minutes, I wanted more. I'll settle for something else though. I'll be cool if this reflection helps introduce the project to just a few more people. So if you haven't heard it, do me a favor and check it out. Then I hope we can share in the joy of *The Sundown*. Okay?

## CHAPTER TEN
### *Set Out in the Dark*
Mighty Theodore
Written by MC Till

Full disclosure. Mighty Theodore creates all our book covers. He came up with that initial blue guy for our first *Boom Bap Review*. He did the follow up green cover, last year's LL Cool J-inspired piece as well as our *Native Tongues Review* cover. So we know him and love his work. Could this review be biased? Yes. Is his new album still dope? Absolutely yes! Also to note is how we work with the Mighty Theodore. We commissioned him for each cover including this book's cover. In no way shape or form did we or do we work with Mighty Theodore or any other artist by trading favors. We paid him for this cover AND we listened to his new album and realized it was one of our favorites. This put us in this unique position where it could be viewed as a conflict of interest. It is not. In fact, Mighty Theodore didn't even know we were going to write this review. He will see it for the first time after the book is published. However, as I stated, I could very well be biased because of our infinity we have toward Mighty Theodore and his art. We ask that you consider all that as you read this review. Furthermore, the bottom line is the music and that's something any and everyone can listen to and form their own opinion. Here is mine...

This album by Mighty Theodore is one of the most soulful albums I've heard this year. His voice alone is pure soul. Whether he is showing off his crooning skills or spitting bars in his low baritone voice, Theodore reveals an old jazzy soul. It's like he was sitting in those Mile Davis quintet sessions with Coltrane, Wayne Shorter, Herbie Hancock, Ron Carter and others just taking it all in. He reappears as the Native Tongues are forming and creating their early masterpieces. He is a fly on the wall during many a D&D session. He takes in all that soul and releases it on the mic. The thing about this particular album is that the musical landscapes match his soul, resulting in one big soul fest wrapped up in some boom bap and definitely Hip-Hop through and through.

The album opens up with dedicating the music to *armies of the night. That real live bunch that comes out after dark. Here is some music with you in mind.* Then the first song "Rebel Vanguard " begins the sultry sounds as Theodore positions the album in nostalgic memories. It feels like a light, reflective vibe, but there is more. Nostalgia is not all fun. During the hook he questions, *Why they want to test me for?* This isn't a Fresh Prince of Bel Air episode where Theodore, from Philadelphia, gets a life in luxury in California. Not even close. Instead, Theodore is left to figure it out. He gets help from a great guest verse provided by Fly Anakin.

"Phantom Riders" follows the same mood as "Rebel Vanguard" almost as a sequel to it. This time Sean Brown provides the guest verse. This is a recurring practice on the album. Theodore brings in a wonderful supporting cast featuring the likes of J Scienide, Brainorchestra, SonnyJim, Hassaan Mackey, and others.

In addition to the soul and the features, *Set Out in the Dark* has a wonderful sequence of skits. One skit samples dialogue about the movie, *The Warriors*. This movie has been quoted and referenced in so many Hip-Hop songs by so many emcees including Ol' Dirty Bastard, Redman, Ice Cube, and many more. This could be viewed as the first "Hip-Hop" movie as it painted a picture of a youth culture that in many ways paralleled a youth culture that gave birth to Hip-Hop. By tying in this dialogue specifically, Mighty Theodore connects the origins of Hip-Hop to his album. It is grounded and rooted in paying homage.

In summary, Mighty Theodore's music is as fresh as his book covers. His approach to art is unique. He draws from different sample sources to create collages that present a certain soulful aesthetic. His music does the same thing. If his artwork had a sound, this album would be it.

## CHAPTER ELEVEN

### *Omowale*
### Wildchild
#### Written by MC Till

Roc Marciano makes dope music. Knowledge the Pirate too. Griselda as well. I could give you a ridiculously long list of rappers in this vein from El Camino to ethemadassasin to Honey Dinero. These are emcees who know how to rhyme. They pick great beats. They make quality albums that have a high quality of dopeness from beginning to end. And they spit lyrics about things I'll never fully understand. There is gun talk, misogynistic references that make me cringe, and slang that I can't fully appreciate. That's not a knock or diss. They are sharing stories that need to be heard. On the flipside, Speech & Arrested Development make dope music. So does Common. Ill Conscious as well. I could give you a rather long list from Awon to Skyzoo to vsteeze to John Robinson and more that provide not only dope albums but also uplifting messages that give the listener some hope. Personally, I want more of that. I want the scales to be tipped towards artists that bring more hopeful messages.

Pause.

Wildchild is not a newcomer to Hip-Hop. I remember hearing him for the first time as a member of Lootpack on their cult classic *Soundpieces: Da Antidote*. If you are into boom bap Hip-Hop and don't know this album, I highly suggest you give it a listen. You can find it just about anywhere now. But that album came out over 20 years ago! Does Wildchild still have it? Can he deliver a quality project two decades after that amazing Lootpack debut? Let's find out.

Play.

Play what? Play the new album, *Omowale,* by Wildchild. This album touches on so many important issues. Wildchild speaks to racial inequality, police brutality, stereotyping, Black fatherhood, and more. He does so over top notch production from beatsmiths like Madlib, Nottz, Georgia Anne Muldrow, and Theory Hazit to name a few. Full disclosure, Theory Hazit and I used to be neighbors (well, we lived like 2 miles from each other) and I consider him a friend: a friend who makes some of the best beats out there. Bias aside, if that's even possible, he is dope. But, go listen to his work and decide for yourself. Okay back to Wildchild.

Well, before we talk about him, let's talk about Georgia Anne Muldrow who had an incredible year. First, she produced that phenomenal album for Elzhi. And here on *Omowale* she provides beats on four of the best songs on the album plus an interlude. First is "PTSD" which might be my favorite song on the album which is weird because it does not feature loud, booming drums that I typically prefer. But, there is something about this song from Ms. Muldrow's voice on the hook, to the low frequency and faint kick drum thumping, to Wildchild himself. Everything works here perfectly for a chilling effect.

So now we go to one of my favorite transitions of any album ever. The song after "PTSD" features Wildchild's son, Miles Brown (which you might know as Jack Johnson from the hit tv show *Blackish*). Miles is arguing that Lebron James is the

G.O.A.T. (Greatest Of All Time) while Wildchild is countering that Michael Jordan is. (Wildchild is right. I mean maybe Lebron technically is a better basketball player like Eminem might technically be a better rapper than say Common or Black Thought, but both of them are better overall IMO. I digress). Now that we are thinking about this father son relationship, Wildchild brings in Big Daddy Kane and Posdnous to create a song about fatherhood over a funky Georgia Anne Muldrow beat. The theme and feel of both songs go hand in hand. It is a perfect 1-2 combo.

Let's stick with honoring Ms. Muldrow on the track "3 Sistas & a Child" where Wildchild raps, *Hold up fellas, my sisters' speaking. Shhhh* and *let's celebrate, show the ladies some love.* Then after one verse he lays out the royal carpet for Dynasty and Medusa to offer the final two verses. Assuming Ms. Muldrow, providing the beat, is the third sista, then the child is Wildchild. Which makes sense considering 'child' is in his stage name. This song speaks to a larger theme of the album: selflessness.

Yes, Wildchild is fully present and very confident. Guest verses withstanding, he shares about himself and his experiences. However, he does so in a way that offers something productive and healthy for the discourse. Remember how I said I wanted the scales to be tipped towards more hopeful messages? Well, that's exactly what we get on *Omowale*. It is 100% Wildchild but it is also 100% for others. He is able to present messages that are for the betterment not just of him but of us, of all of us. He does this while simultaneously inviting us into vulnerability and a great party with a beautiful soundtrack. Although some of the lyrical content is dense, the beats are funky and fun. We can dance and vibe out to something beautiful and positive.

So what are you waitin' for? Search *Omowale* by Wildchild, press play, and enjoy the positive vibes.

Part Three
# AN ESSAY
# SOME LINER NOTES
# &
# A DEDICATION

## CHAPTER TWELVE
### Who you Callin' a B***h?
#### Written by MC Till

I am often torn. I love Hip-Hop music. I also really enjoy letting people be who they are. I used to judge people often. But, over time I realized that it is much better to appreciate people without judgment. Living this way feels great. I don't have to be responsible for what you or anyone else says or does. I can definitely be here for people and I can offer my perspective when invited to do so. However, I don't have to be the guy who decides what's best for everyone I meet.

I also don't have to be the guy who decides what is or isn't appropriate for a rapper to say in a song or on an album. And this is where I'm torn. Sometimes emcees report on what they see and I love that kind of Hip-Hop. Other times an emcee will tell a story or paint colorful pictures with similes and metaphors. I really appreciate just about any style of Hip-Hop. However there are a few things that I have a hard time digesting and I'd like to open up a conversation about two of those things: lyrics filled with unnecessary and irredeemable violence or misogyny.

I'll be listening to an album and all of a sudden the emcee drops the word b***h. Even though I don't like to judge people, let's go ahead and do that. Let's say the emcee doesn't know any better. Ignorance. This judgment at least brings about some empathy. Like what happened to this guy to where he just casually drops that word? Let's assume another judgment. Cultural. It is not ignorant. It is not even used in the perceived negative way that I view it. Instead the emcee more or less uses the word as a term of endearment. Is this far-fetched? Well it definitely doesn't feel right but does that mean it is wrong? The last option I think about is the simple right vs wrong and the emcee is wrong. I can see moments where using what I would call an extreme word like this is necessary or at least thoughtfully intentional. The emcee might be trying to convey a message and this word is the best way to do that. Maybe the emcee is playing a character. Perhaps the emcee also believes using this word is wrong, but is necessary to complete the song. I can imagine many instances where an emcee would use the word in an intentional way, not meant to be degrading but instead meant to portray a reality or emotion that only that word can convey. I may not agree, but I can at least appreciate the motive.

Regardless of any of that, I still don't feel right when I hear what to me are blatant misogynistic lyrics. Again, my personal feelings don't make it wrong, but it does give me pause. And honestly, I don't always know what to do about it.

One thing I've been thinking about a lot lately is women in Hip-Hop. Even in this book, you don't see many albums written and performed by women. Why? When I search around for new boom bap albums to listen to every week I don't see a lot of albums performed by female emcees. Why is that? Am I looking in the wrong places? Are women underrepresented in the boom bap world?

So I co-author books, put out virtual magazines, co-host a podcast, moderate daily conversations online, and more. What is my responsibility? How do I become a better listener? What are the right questions to ask of you, the reader and listener? What are the right questions to ask myself? How do I turn from being part of the problem to becoming a part of the solution?

What do you think? Part of our DNA here at Everybody's Hip-Hop is community. There is no way I can ask better questions and explore better answers than if I ask it with you. So, I ask you to reflect on what I just shared and offer your thoughts. I'm here, ready to listen.

## A Note About Liner Notes

When I was a kid I loved buying new tapes. When I got a little older I loved buying new CDs. Part of the excitement was looking at the artwork and reading the liner notes! Not every album came with them so when they did, it was such a treat. With all the digital releases and limited run digipaks and such, we don't get to enjoy liner notes as much anymore. Well, we are out to change that. As I've mentioned in previous books, I can't stand complaining. I like to act. So we are introducing a new segment of our books called "Liner Notes." Pretty creative name right? Haha, but seriously, we invited select artists to provide liner notes for this publication. We did not give them guidance on how long or short their reflections should be. Like they do with their music, they were free to create and write whatever they wanted. We love this idea and are really excited about it. We'll see how it goes. Let us know what you think. Do you like them? Anything you would change or like to hear from artists around their albums? Let us know something. And with that, here are liner notes to a few of our favorite albums this year written by the artists themselves.

# CHAPTER THIRTEEN
## *Words to the Wise*
### Vic Monroe & Tone Spliff
Liner notes by Tone Spliff, approved by Vic Monroe

"Wise Words from Bazz"
Big shout to Baz for blessing the introduction of our album. We wanted some meaningful spoken word/knowledge and Baz delivered.

"Words to the Wise"
We both agreed to start the project off with this joint. More of a mellow vibe, but still powerful. This one features the amazing vocalist, The ONE Lavic.

"Destinations (feat. GQ)"
Vic and I were discussing features for the project. We didn't want to have too many, and decided on just two. We also wanted brand new emcees that weren't on our EP *Marinade* (shout to Freddie Black, Innocent? & Milano Constantine who were on that). GQ is a more recent emcee that got on my radar being on 9th Wonder's label Jamla Records. I felt this beat would be perfect for him, and I reached out on IG and chopped up the business. He agreed, I gave him the theme, and both GQ and Vic killed this.

"Prosperous"
This is one that gives me chills. I love everything about this one. Vic's rhymes, the eerie sample/beat, the AZ "Rather Unique" sample I threw in on the first verse lol. I love songs with a good story, and Vic brought just that.

"Kiddos Skit"
Vic had this audio. It's his kids getting on Vic about not being famous on TV or the radio. I told him he has to ground them for that. Haha. But this set the perfect tone (no pun intended) for the next song.

"Ain't Sayin' Nothin'"
This is probably the most hype song on the album. Right from the jump its drums smack people in their face. Real simple sample/loop, and a dope Jeru the Damaja phrase for the cut. This has one of my favorite opening lines from Vic, *James Worthy in a Michigan jersey, the flow ugly.* That bar gives me an instant stank face.

"As We Proceed"
It's just like that, as we proceed! This is that RAW Hip-Hop. We (are) letting the listeners know we're back, we're still dope (if not doper), and the plan hasn't changed. We (are) preserving that sound with this one.

"In The World (feat. Recognize Ali)"
Recognize Ali is the 2nd emcee we got for this project. Vic contacted him with the beat and arranged it all. Me and Rec have worked numerous times already, so this came together nicely. This one has gotten the most love I think with all the Hip-Hop shows I follow.

"Broken Heart Diploma (skit)"
R.I.P. Richard Pryor. Vic and I are both fans. Vic had the idea of using this quick skit before the next song.

"Visions of Love"

I think all of my projects have a girl song. Something the ladies can vibe with. This is that song. Probably one of my recent favorite beats. Soulful. Vic kills it as usual. It's hard to pick a favorite lol.

"Time Goes Bye"
This joint is a smoothie. I felt it was good to place towards the end to give the listener that feeling of the album coming to an end soon, but not to lose interest just yet.

"Food For Thought"
We were considering naming the album *Food For Thought*, but decided not to (good thing cause Che Noir dropped an album with that title immediately after). I think this was one of the first songs we recorded for the project and it ended up being the closer. And one hell of a closer it is. After Vic gave his words to the wise, we left everyone with food for thought.

## CHAPTER FOURTEEN
*Listen to the Masters*
Ghettosocks & DK
Liner Notes by Ghettosocks & DK

"Reflections"
This is the first collaboration that we had both worked on and felt that we needed to have this here to start the album off properly.

"What It Seems"
Ghettosocks' verse discusses the concept of blind patriotism recorded originally in late 2019. Our goal was really to capture what was going on around us at the time.

"The Masters"
The goal was to find emcees that could compliment Ghettosocks and DK who were bonafide masters in their field.

"Be A Mango"
DK made the beat which was originally called "You've got to be a man" which inspired Socks to flip the title to "Be a Mango" as a starting point to discuss toxic masculinity. To expand on this concept the skills of Phoenix Pagliacci and LXVNDR were generously shared to provide additional perspective. Once the lyrics were done, DK added a few small elements such as vocal samples and horns which made the song danceable.

"All In"
Talks about goal setting. This song features production by Moka Only and DK.

"Industry Skit"
A skit that jokingly talks about how Hip-Hop/rap music is not taken seriously in Halifax, and for Canada as a whole, for that matter. We wanted to present a dismissive music industry person who had no idea what they were talking about. The skit was inspired from the comedic stylings of The Jerky Boys of the '90s.

"Chicken Chop"
Following up the skit with the toughest beat on the project, DK had met UFO Fev in NYC during a trip and felt he would fit on this joint with Sipset veterans, Tachichi and Ghettosocks. "Chicken Chop" was also inspired by a local eatery by the same name where we go frequently.

"Smoove Regardless"
Ghettosocks became a household name in Halifax after being featured on Jay Bizzy's track "Help! I Got Robbed!" In 2007. He really stole the show on that one and talked about how he wasn't the one being robbed, rather he was the one doing the robbing. He had a great line in that song that said *being broke was hard, but I was smooth regardless* so we decided to use that line for the hook, where he complimented it with some classic Slick Rick vocals.

"John McEnroe"
Discusses current events such as police brutality, the residential school systems as well as performative activism. The beat contains a saxophone sample with a serious tone to it. Our goal was to put together serious subject matter that matched the feeling of the saxophone.

"Baggage"

The last song on here that features just both of us. I wanted the beat to have a storytelling vibe that made it feel like the listener was reading chapters in a fiction novel. Halifax-based big band leader, James Shaw, who is known to push the boundaries of big band jazz, adds saxophone parts to add another dynamic.

Editor's note: Go get the album *Listen to the Masters* by searching that same title on Bandcamp.

# CHAPTER FIFTEEN
## *Infinite Wisdom*
### Awon & SOUL.DOPE.95
#### Liner Notes by Awon

Side A

1. Infinite Wisdom ft. Napoleon Da Legend
2. The Chosen
3. Timeline
4. Union ft. Tiff The Gift
5. You'll Never
6. Stolen Peace
7. Thrones for Sale (Side B, begins with track 7)
8. Have You Guessin' ft. God King Preach
9. Sophisticated Information
10. Pastor Troy
11. Baldwin Reprise ft. Anti-Lilly
12. Park Bench ft. Dephlow
13. Sohi ft. Sin (Bonus)

Mixed and mastered by SOUL.DOPE.95 at the The Dope Spot Studios in Los Angeles, California

Soul
And
Dope
I = 9th letter of alphabet
E = 5th letter of the alphabet

For Sadie, his mother.

Artwork by:

Dathan Kane
@_dkane

Recorded by Antwan Wiggins in Alexandria, Virginia

A & R Cortez Whitehead aka Dugga

Executive Producer: Phoniks for Don't Sleep Records

About the album:

*Infinite Wisdom* was recorded over the course of the past year and created completely over the internet. Rashard Whitehead aka Dugga, happened to come across the mysterious producer, SOUL.DOPE.95 while scrolling beat videos and sounds on Instagram. After reaching out to SOUL.DOPE.95 he connected him with Awon and instantly a chemistry was born. Bonding over fatherhood and music the pair seemed to know one another without ever speaking over the phone. SOUL.DOPE.95 infamously does not own a cellphone and only operates online and through email. After months of file sharing back and forth, Infinite Wisdom has come to life. This body of work is an exploration of Blackness and the standing of African Americans (and) also Africans living in the diaspora in popular culture. There are many recurring themes that question Blackness, heritage, love, and a mental resolution to break generational trauma through positive self images. It is more of a reflective celebration which sounds thoughtful and liberating. The production offers flavors of jazz, soul, and gospel to create the sonic gumbo that pairs well with Awon's introspective approach to writing. The duo hopes to share this celebration with the world and invites everyone to listen in and learn. The artwork for the album is an actual painting owned by Awon created by the burgeoning artist Dathan Kane titled "1988" after the graffiti tag of Awon. The mood is one that is warped and represents the artist's abstract interpretation of warped vinyl. This is a nod to the celebration of heritage as Dathan is also an artist of color operating in a space where many African Americans are not recognized.

Here is a track-by-track breakdown of the album.

"Infinite Wisdom" ft. Napoleon Da Legend is the opener of the album as well as the title track. This record is the blueprint of what the listener can expect from the rest of the album. It was written as an educational tool through experience. Napoleon and I serve as street professors schooling the listeners on Black history through popular culture as well as African American History as it should be taught in books. This is a rebuttal to the so-called rejection of critical race theory being taught in K-12 schools by the extreme right. The sale of "wokeness" is also touched on so the person on the receiving end knows that this is not a drill. This album is going to be an experience of Black expression that goes deep.

"The Chosen" is a celebration of my own independent achievement in music. It is a song meant to inspire those who are trying to make it. I wrote about the people who helped me along the way, but the star of the record are those who are the people who make it possible - the people who showed me love. As independent artists with no commercial backing we sought out our own gigs. We are the managers and executives. We get to see first hand the reactions of people around the world in the places we have been. It's always been warm, it's always been dope, so the goal is not to let anyone else tell you differently. See the impact you can make for yourself on your own, through your eyes. Celebrate your victories even if they are small.

"Timeline" is a record that came about early in the recording process. It was a beat that struck me as being different for me and out of my comfort zone, but it also felt jazzy and somewhat highbrow. My goal lyrically was to take a modern flow and own it. I also wanted to add some color on fronting online which is getting many young people incarcerated. A lot is made of lyrics these days as we see in the case that is being made against YSL (Young Stoner Life Records) members in Georgia. Many rappers are fighting for freedom of speech, but many rappers are also speaking directly to crimes they committed in raps. With that juxtaposition it's a crazy time to be an emcee, so I made a record about all the cap, the fronting, and unnecessary incrimination I see on my timeline.

"Union" featuring Tiff the Gift is the rap version of *Married With Children* as she is my wife, but also a beast with the bars. There is a lot to be made about this red pill, beta male, alpha male stuff online and I touched on that a bit. I feel like those topics are quite divisive and I just wanted to bring some humor and light to what a successful relationship could be like.

"You'll Never" is just braggadocio all the way. I used a lot of Marvel references and sci-fi references throughout. I even dropped a Rick and Morty reference in there. I'm a fan of all that stuff and it's my way of incorporating pop culture into the music in a way that still fits in with my narrative on the album. SOUL.DOPE.95 chose a dope sample at the end of this as well. It's the nuances, the samples, and the sequencing that ties this altogether.

"Stolen Peace" reflects on my stolen youth due to making bad choices and some of the circumstances around me. It's basically about stealing youth from yourself by growing up too fast. I wanted to take some accountability for my life and on this record I lay out the true stories of my upbringing as well as my own decisions that informed my perspective today. Hopefully people can learn from my mistakes and take some of these jewels away from this to balance their own lives.

Side B begins with "Thrones for Sale"
This one is deep, we often use the word "king" when greeting one another, but that term is used too loosely in my opinion because those claiming "king" or that they are "kings" are not conducting themselves that way in their households or in their communities. It becomes toxic masculinity and I get the term thrones for sale because everyone seems to have a price these days. They sell their dignity for cheap for material gain while true wealth comes from your deeds and impact on earth.

This brings us into "Have You Guessin'" featuring God King Preach of the Indigo Klan. This record is a compare and contrast of perspectives about carrying a weapon. I have an older perspective of hustling and understanding the consequences of my decisions to carry. Hoping that a shooting in self-defense doesn't come with a conviction etc, while Preach uses his losses of friends and "beefs" as his reasons for carrying. It all comes back to everyone just wanting to make it home and if you decide to pick up a gun, understand what it means and the power that is behind it.

"Sophisticated Information" is another braggadocio record colored differently because it reflects on my experience in rap. It also utilizes double entendres and references to luxury brands and sports to create the narrative. Here I focus on being unknown to the masses but also known by the masses. It's about being the type of emcee that if you know you know. It's about being happy with being the "emcee's emcee." The sample is something SOUL.DOPE.95 found that discusses the Dogon, an African Tribe that possesses sophisticated information. I feel like this reflects how people don't understand how we do it in the underground and still have success.

"Pastor Troy" is a record I made with my late grandmother Newzella in mind. I remember her vividly telling me I should be a preacher, but if I rap at least tell the truth. So her giving me her blessing to become an emcee is akin to being a Pastor like Troy. It's a play on words and a rap reference to a Dirty South legend. I actually met him in the airport in Atlanta. He is a really cool brother. I grew up in a religious household. My grandmother was a Seventh Day Adventist: there were lots of rules. I don't eat meat right now, ha ha. Although I'm not a part of that church, my grandmother was big on spiritual exploration and building a relationship with God as long as you made an effort to have one. Rest in power to my grandmother Newzella.

"Baldwin (Reprise)" featuring Anti-Lilly continues the conversation we began on my solo album *Soulapowa* from 2019. This record is an exploration of black identity and what it is to be African American living in the diaspora. The ideas I expressed are the feeling of fitting in nowhere as we have no national identity, or do we? This record is probably one of my most complex and compelling because of the brutal honesty involved in its creation. Anti-Lilly, my brother, was ferocious and honest on this one. It's a special record to me overall.

"Park Bench" featuring Dephlow is a record about soaking up game. This record is about adapting to your situation, evolving daily, and letting your spirit guide you to a path of righteousness. This one is a reflection of the past that informs my present and in turn creates my future. To me this record is the culmination of the themes of the album. It also serves as the epic closer as the album technically comes to an end on a high note. Dephlow comes through with a riveting verse from his perspective and experience and ideas of reckoning.

"SoHi" featuring Sin is a bonus cut on the album. Sonically SOUL.DOPE.95 gave this a soulful, yet jazzy tone. I was moved by the vocal sample and used the lyrics as a play on the words 'so high.' I decided to tell a story about when keeping it real goes wrong. On the second verse Sin speaks on alcohol as a vice and also celebrates life through finding a balance and not over-indulging. That concludes *Infinite Wisdom*, a soulful expression of Blackness.

# CHAPTER SIXTEEN
*Down in the Rabbit Hole*
DJ Parental & Mattic
Liner Notes by Mattic

The Album

One day I got an inbox from a producer from Paris named DJ Parental asking if I was down to do a joint project with him. I normally don't answer these sorta emails, because though I get plenty, I believe in just working with family on music and I'm big on the human element for sound creation. We have to get along or gel with each other to make good music. That's very important to me, plus I'm very busy creating in my own world. But this day I was feeling good and although it was an email, I felt the vibe from him. So I said let me check out what you are doing because I wasn't familiar with his music. I checked out his projects with Pete Flux, Horror City, and Carter P and was digging them. He then sent me a file of beats and I loved them. Very mellow, sample-based, and full of ambient colors, but the biggest factor was I didn't have anything in my beat vaults that sounded like his music, so I agreed. I also noted to him that I add in many things over production such as extra samples, vocal samples, delays, echoes, skits and dialogues from a vast amount of sources I have collected for years. I don't just write and rhyme. I don't separate it either. It's all together with the rhyming in one big style package I call The Ghost In The Machine. He agreed and everything was set to begin.

After over 2 years, we got to know each other from afar and came up with 12 tracks and entitled it "Down In The Rabbit Hole." The title is based on just where my thinking, life, and soul are these days; deep in my own rabbit hole where I can process information I gather, stay to myself, my family, and in my universe doing my passion of just creating anything with rules that I can think of away from the outside world in peace. It was also during the time of the pandemic so being around people was a no no. We did the whole album remotely from our own studios and even though we live 2 hours by train from each other, to this day we have never met in person. I'm hard to catch up with, but hopefully by the time this is issued we will have met. Parental is a cool guy - my brother who makes fantastic music and is easy to work with. So here's a breakdown of the songs.

"Down In The Rabbit Hole"

I had been watching Alice In Wonderland with my son and totally had forgotten how ill this animation was until I revisited it. It made perfect sense with what and how I was feeling about life and how I viewed my hidden universe: not normal, discovering things and creating sound from all that intake. I also at that time had been watching *The Matrix* and spending my days listening to old Alan Watts lectures, so my perspective on life was changing deeply at a rapid speed which also plays into my writing. I write using a simple yet complex format I call Autism Lyricism, where it's artistically influenced by my son who is autistic. Studying him has also changed my life and my creativity in a huge way; just breaking the traditional function of how we've been programmed to do and view things. It's like a rewired layout but still wired with spontaneous thoughts, but they just cross differently. Normal rhyming, but different. The intersection of simple and complex mixture while riding the beats. Parental's dark and melodic compositions are just perfect to build upon. So this is the introduction of us and where we are - *Down In The Rabbit Hole*.

"Ghost Machine"

When I first arrived in France, I was called "the Machine", because of my output in the studio with tracks. Back then I could do multiple tracks in hours or a whole album in a couple of days. But that was many moons ago, and with time it has changed. I was always fond of this name, but as I got older things started to make a different sense to me. I started to think that if the body is a machine, then what lies within it is the soul which I call the ghost. I mean once a person has passed, humans have always been fond of referring to the formless dead as a ghost, but it's just a soul trapped on earth with no body roaming around. So while I am here, one of my aliases is the Ghost in the Machine. (It means) the self that is the unspoken heard, doing what the universe does, which is create. This beat is also special because it's a strong combination of Parental & his partner-in-crime, a producer also from Paris named Alcynoos. It's as smooth and cool as the other side of the pillow. They make a wonderful team. It also has live guitars from Haken Besik and Samuel Tournier. It's a heater. This track is about feeling the reality of what's commanding the machine - your soul.

"Lost Exit Door"

Really love this beat; nice dark sample with well balanced drums. I was watching *Menace To Society* one afternoon. The scenes with O-Dog, Cain, and the guys on the couch talking sh*t made me reminisce about life back in Charlotte, NC. I came up as a teen with guys like that, always talking sh*t, but it was love. Well at least from most of them. I wasn't that kind of guy, but I always got a kick out of it and was always listening and laughing without becoming the next target for them. But of course they would get me too. It built tough skin for your personality. If I was going talk sh*t, it would be in emceeing. I came from a generation where your ego was letting people know how nice or ill you were. That could be directly or indirectly. This I would say is directly boasting for fun. Just a exit door from yourself that you go through sometimes and become another entity. That's kinda lost nowadays or executed so wrong that people are losing their lives over it or making it a spectacle to drive record sales. Shame, but that's life. So that is why I named it "Lost Exit Door." Losing yourself for a moment.

"Flight Of The Albatross"

Sometimes I find myself watching, studying some of the most crazy and interesting (to me) documentaries. Not only to teach myself but for pure enjoyment mainly. The data will process automatically. One day I was watching a documentary on birds at sea and it came to the albatross. First I loved the name, but then I was just amazed by the daily activities of this bird; flying and gliding for hundreds of miles over the sea or ocean without stopping. They are huge and no other animals really mess with them. I live in the harbor by the English Channel. It's right below the hills I live in so it's a 10 minute walk to get there. I was walking along the coast one day looking out to sea, enjoying the view and deep in my imagination thinking how cool it would be if I saw an albatross fly over. I was listening to this track of Parental's and it just went with the moment. The smooth tone of the sax was reminding me of the brisk wind and the horns reminded me of the waves motioning back and forth. The albatross flies alone or in groups. I myself am mostly alone and sometimes (rarely) with crew, but always flying in my imagination. So I took the idea of being the albatross; a big bird flying over a body of madness for miles caught in its imagination and displaying it. I think Hip-Hop has had a multitude of deaths and one of them is Imagination. Mostly everyone completely mimics another man's success and even if you rhyme about what your environment surrounds you with, not many paint with an imagination. It baffles me, because I am in my own imagination for a majority of the days and nights since being a child. Oh yea, I also took a Erykah Badu chorus from one of her songs, flipped the words, and sung them in the same melody as her for this track. I'm just a big bird flying over this world of madness alone or with a rare few exploring in my imagination.

"Fly Guys & Black Widows" Ft Yagomeans

My brother YagoMeans, fellow Kinship from Charlotte NC, is a very good brother. We have known each other for a long time. We think alike while still being individuals. We respect each other and always share information that could possibly help with growth in this life. Plus he's one of the illest MCs I personally know. Very crafty with the words. I sent this Parental banger which reminds me of an old '80s joint with this face-banging guitar slap sample and airy groove. I asked him to set this joint off as it was one of the last songs to record for the album. Thought I'd let him take the lead and feed off his energy because I completely trust his mind in writing. What I got back was a verse talking about a guy feeling good about himself on an evening out where nothing could go wrong. It actually sounded like one of his rare nights out in the city of Charlotte. So instead of matching him with more fly guy talk, I decided to twist things up and take the transition into when the guy he was rhyming about arrived home to a relationship he (and the woman) was fed up with. Again you have to understand this album was made during the pandemic and this particular track was when things were in the beginning stages of when places were opening back up, including nightlife. I started to understand that the pandemic ended a lot of relationships due to the fact that people were stuck with each other for weeks, breaking their routines of going to work, seeing friends, shopping, clearing the mind, and just basically having a break from each other. Some couples dealt with it just fine or became stronger in unity and some clashed with it, starting to see that the person they thought they were in love with wasn't the right person for them. This period really gave an inside understanding if you and your mate were more than lovers. It tested the subject of being friends which is the main key to keeping a long lasting relationship. It's two perspectives of a guy out away from his kingdom feeling free and fly about himself and returning home to the reality of a relationship turned into a stressful nightmare. This is all from the guy's point of view. *You was fly, but got caught. Sucked dry and left high. Bit by them things, a black widow sings.*

"Gods Mirror"

Elegant egotism. As a person, each day due to my studies, I get in tune with the "Self," the unseen force behind who you think you are. But before, as everyone else, I was only in tune with who we think we are such as John, David, Mary or whoever we have been named, told and educated on who we are. As a person grows, and I'll take an artist in this case, we create different personas to revamp ourselves and not get bored. In rhyming we sometimes create a character that is other than ourselves and a bit higher due to the talent we have tapped into. As said before, I came from an origin where you bragged and showed how nice you were with the words and how you presented them, "Like check me or this out." So to this day I keep that in the bag. It's just confidence in your skill level. I believe we are all the universe having a human experience here on earth. We are all Gods (and devils) of our doings. Not so much as an entity that masters over all with judgment and decision over everyones faith, but just of yourself. Wherever you go with that is up to you and you alone. You can grow it and apply more knowledge to your daily actions for better or let it run wild throughout your ups and downs during this adventure. Heaven and hell is all around us. I like to think of this Parental production as a stroll around your garden in your own heaven, watching the life manifest within it. (It's) taking a moment of boasting amongst one's self. In this case it's boasting about your skill or how nice you are. This action for me these days only comes out when rhyming....sometimes and this is one of those times. Proud of what you do and how you, as a student, have mastered it. In the mirror of your garden showing off to yourself. Just don't let it stay with you everywhere you go. As you walk away from the mirror allow it to also walk away from you as it does when you leave from in front of it.

"Miles To Go"

No matter how hard the road becomes, you have to keep ahead. You have to get as far as you can. Along this journey you are most definitely going to encounter elements that come in many forms to influence you. What sticks with you and what you resonate with is only and solely up to you. But again you have to keep going physically and mentally. I am influenced by a lot of things and I am thankful for having the mind, interest, and pull to intake and filter what makes me tick differently. I love it, and one of the outlets for it is writing. If everyone is going right, I'm going left. That ain't for everyone and I more than gladly accept that. I love it and that's all that matters. But I do see the path most are engaging and I often speak on it or flip it to a comparison in ability of the skill. Anyway, it's a soft motion tempo style of production blessed by Parental and I wanted to approach it in a manner of moving through these miles, but noticing those also in movement or stuck. I also attempted to sing during the chorus. In the past I always went with other talented singers whom I had met and developed a relationship with artistically and humanly. But sometimes waiting on people is like waiting for babies to be born. So I decided to do it myself. People I can't sang, but on the other hand I'm free to do whatever I want on my music. With the help of some reverb and vocal phone and my amazing sound man Julien who mixes and masters all my music, it came out alright...for me haha. Also the chorus is saying I have come to show you the way and that way is to be yourself. Just be yourself.

"Galactic Elevation" Ft Gt Lovecraft

During the pandemic I started to make music with a group called ASM (A State Of Mind), GT Lovecraft, FP, and producer Rhino. We, along with another producer named Daylight Robbery who I have another group with called Odd Holiday, created a super group called Clouds In A Headlock. With these groups we created a crew called Offkiltr. I really love these guys as humans, friends and bros and respect their talents in music. We basically get together and make some off-the-wall Hip-Hop and as far as the emcees, we test each other in a brotherhood way on the mic to take our writing to the next level. Nerdy rap lol. I have watched these emcees grow from teens to men. I connect deeply with GT on a human level and he is also one of the nicest emcees I personally know. We also have a group together in the crew called Endgame with a producer named Pitch92. This song is an example of taking each other to the next level. Feeding off each other's creative output and writing; connected together, going galactic in patterns over the track. This Parental beat was originally an interlude, but I loved it so much that I asked him to extend it for a song. Sometimes interludes are a short moment that actually could have been a dope song. It reminded me of a child-like feeling of when I was young and of my son running around the garden with his friends feeling so free and full of life. Writing with GT gives that feeling too, we just let it all out with our inner child modes of fun.

"Reflection Of Escapism"

As a kid and teen in my hometown of Charlotte NC, I came up in different hoods. With hard work and blessings I watched my parents go from ground zero to a nice middle class life by the time I left the States. I had no brothers or sisters, just me. I didn't get everything I wanted but having both parents I got everything I needed. My parents kept a firm grip on me with education and fear. I also can look back on those days and see that I was always different from others. Man, I knew and seen some sh*t during those early years: sports athletes, the girl-next-door, fools, smart guys, drug dealers, flamboyant dudes, sh*t talkers, hoes, slick talkers, liars, killers, weak people, strong folks, and the wise. You name it, I've seen and encountered it all. This is how I developed energy resonating from feeling and viewing who I was around. I have seen some stuff and by the grace of the universe, I never got caught up in mischief. One, I was terrified of disappointing my parents, and two, I wasn't going to get into most of that stuff because I could witness the highs and lows and effects it was causing on the people around me. Once I left those hoods, especially the neighborhood I came up in during my teen years, I'd swing back around to slide through and kick it with my bros

I kept in touch with. Talking and burning weed together. Some of them would always tell me about myself saying back then they didn't understand me or get how I was moving. Always going left, but as we got older they would say they were proud of me and who I had become. I didn't let the ways of the hood touch me while living in it. I escaped it. This Parental track reminds me of those days, wandering around the apartment complexes or the neighborhood streets I lived on, absorbing and filtering what was going on around me. I'm just rhyming it in a left riddle format - the format I developed in life that has taken me to where I am and live and do in the now. I am reflecting on the escape.

"Level 10 (Rage)"

This Parental track struck me as a graceful two-step into an orbit of rage. It could be the grounded motion flow of the piano sample or the busy drum pattern under it. Maybe it's both. The beat made me feel like we are coming through and there is nothing you can do to stop it. It's not so much what I'm saying that relates with rage, but it's the placement of the added samples in the chorus and the turning of the delays and feedback to the max. The demo is even crazier. It's the quest to your level 10 and maintaining yourself and the skill through an insane episode of sound. I took a Q-Tip chorus just to hint that no you can't stop it and no you can't get caught in it ever. When you fail, go back and try again, and if you come back, I'm impressed and will be the first one to shake your hand.

"Satellite Recording"

This was the first track that Parental sent to me before the file of beats for the album. It was the first track that made me know that this is going to happen. We are going to do a project together. It was also the first track recorded. Something about that swing of the piano and the snap of the snare with the bounce of the drums made me know that this guy is damn good. He painted this beat perfectly. I just wanted to have fun with it. Test the waters and dive in full steam, swimming all over and inside the beat. I am a big lover of space, what's going on in it and what we have put in it, so that's why I went with the name "Satellite Recording." I'm in my universe with this beat sending lyrics from my studio (satellite). Transmitting flows in Doctor Outer mode, which is another one of my aliases. I guess it's him making an appearance. It might be track 11, but it's the intro to Parental and I becoming a team.

"Home Cooking"

My God, I am thankful for having my home studio. I call it Winterfell from Game Of Thrones because I live in the north west of Normandy, France. So thankful. When I was in Charlotte doing music with my old crew, I was the only member that didn't have a lab to record. I just didn't have the money to do it. So I would have beats and just write and even if I didn't have beats, I just wrote rhymes all day at home or at work. I would have to go to someone's home studio and record as much as I could before we got tired and passed out or until they decided to put me out. Then it started to become, "Well today I'm not home or I'm with my girl, or I have to work today." You know waiting to record has its ups and downs to it. The ups are that you can have the time to remember and perfect the tracks, but the downs are that it's not the same as it was when you wrote it and due to time the feeling has passed. That energy isn't like it first was. It can happen like that sometimes. Fast forward to arriving in France, my wife, who I met over here and started living with, is a cello player and composer, so when I moved in she already had equipment and knowledge of how to record everything. So she started to record me. We had some long days of sitting together recording endless amounts of songs for hours. Until one day I asked her if we could record and she kinda looked at me with a tired expression and said, "You know what? Today you're going to learn how to record yourself." I was kinda offended at that moment but wasn't going to make an issue about it. So she sat me down that afternoon and from that day taught me the magic that changed my life as an artist - how to record. Till this day it is my love that I can't and don't wish to let go of. Through time we built together a room full of sound that you can escape the outer world from and do whatever comes to mind. These days almost everyone who does music has a home studio to retreat to and dwell in. Parental has his and I have mine. It is how we connected and came up with these tracks remotely, thus home cooking these words and sounds into music.

So that's the breakdown of this album; how we made it and what inspired the 12 songs on it. At the end, there are no words that truly or fully explain the process of creating. I like to end it by saying.....it's all just one big happening......Thank you very much.

## CHAPTER SEVENTEEN
### Paten Locke Tribute
Written by Dillon Maurer

It was the summer of 2017. Paten Locke hopped in his Nissan minivan, aptly named 'A Ride Called Quest' and drove from his record-filled home in Jacksonville, FL to my lobster-filled home here in East Point, GA to put the finishing touches on some of Paten's music. We didn't know it at the time, but that trip and the sessions that sprung from it would turn out to be critical in sculpting Paten's life's work and defining his musical legacy. We really just got up for the jokes though and the music was secondary. If you knew P, he was all about them LOLz.

Of course in true Paten fashion, it wasn't just ONE album we were finishing but TWO. And oh yeah, P didn't quite know which tracks would go to which project but we could 'figure it out along the way'. I was mortified but not surprised. Paten was a consummate overachiever who always set out to redefine the gold standard - why not do it twice at the same time?!

So there we were, polishing *Americancer* + *Dance on My Grave* - without any knowledge of exactly how prophetic those album titles were. Yes, you read that correctly. Years before Paten's cancer diagnosis turned our worlds upside down and took him from us, P was already preparing us (and himself?) for his transition without even knowing. Words hold weight, and those specific words weighed a TON.

Fast forward to 2021 - Paten has been gone for two years and I've spent countless hours compiling music files, recording sessions, & every artifact I could glean from Paten's ancient laptops (P was a true luddite!) in order to present his vision(s) to the world. I was terrified. I wanted so badly to carry out my task with stoic execution but I was overcome with grief every time I took a listen to the music or a look at the artwork. But still - adjustments had to be made, as well as difficult choices about which song would land on which project. (THAT part!) I scoured a multitude of track lists that Paten wrote on his devices; all meticulously...different. I prayed on it. I cried about it. I meditated. Sent smoke signals. ALL that. Guided by P's spirit, we made decisions, and we put 'em on wax!

Perhaps *Americancer* will soon be redefined through the lens of its companion project, *Dance on My Grave* - which will be unveiled in due time. Until then, we can love it for what it is: a masterclass from the triple threat. Paten is entirely in his element chopping up rare & obscure vinyl records, lacing them with chunky, dusty drums and then proceeding to rap & scratch with purpose & precision. The skull-cracking beats range from triumphant to tragic & everything in between. A steadfast cynic, Paten's rhymes run amok as he bounces between dropping gems of knowledge & philosophy to bullying you with braggadocio - always delivering with his trademark sardonic wit and the utmost of confidence. Paten even explores different genres on the record, dabbling in psychedelic rock as a means of displaying his versatility and love for ALL music. (Norwegian Death Metal - check. 1960s Surf Guitar - check. Obscure regional Gospel - double check!)

I was in the final stages of getting the record together, searching for an overall theme to use as a vehicle for presentation when one jumped out at me and smacked me in the face. 'Erudite Eremite'.

er·u·dite (Latin - adjective) - having or showing great knowledge or learning.

er·e·mite (Latin - noun) - a hermit or recluse.

While growing up in Boston, Paten was invited to attend the internationally acclaimed & highly prestigious, Roxbury Latin School. Founded in 1645, Roxbury Latin is the oldest school in continuous existence in North America.

Of course Paten was a star at the school and developed a proficient skill set in the lost language. His love for Latin - the ancient & obscure - was exemplified in his approach to music and an integral part of his identity. The phrase 'Erudite Eremite' is Paten's own Latin rhyme & remains on his Twitter profile to this day as his 2-word autobiography. Not to mention it is now forever immortalized in the Americancer song, 'Wrong Soup':

*The Erudite Eremite - every step's serious*

That's Paten. An artist & soul who had an incredible knowledge. He was willing to share it if you were worthy and equally as passionate. Otherwise, he mostly kept to himself. Unless his daughter, Asha was calling...

-Dillon Maurer // FULL PLATE

## Part Four
# RETROSPECTIVES

## CHAPTER EIGHTEEN
*Paid in Full* – Eric B & Rakim
35 Years Later
Written by Profound

If you sit around with your friends and debate about classic Hip-Hop albums, then you'll be able to relate to this reflection. The first album from Eric B. & Rakim, *Paid in Full,* is a certified classic in the eyes and ears of most Hip-Hop enthusiasts. It's hard to believe it's been 35 years since Eric B & Rakim took not only Hip-Hop, but the world by storm. Originally released July 7$^{th}$, 1987, *Paid in Full* instantly elbowed its way to the forefront of a rapidly growing list of classic Hip-Hop albums. Summer 1987… I can remember it like it was yesterday. It was 10 p.m. Saturday night and I'm buried deep in my room waiting for the weekend Hip-Hop radio show - Chicago's own "The Rap Down." The show, hosted by personalities Ramon-Ski Love, Disco Dave, and Pink-House, was the only place I could hear Hip-Hop on the radio. See, Chicago was and still is big on "House Music," so to finally get access to a radio station that devoted a specific time for Hip-Hop was like Christmas every weekend for this 12 yr. old.

I remember one Saturday night sitting in my room impatiently waiting for 10 p.m. so I could record the show as I normally did to play my favorite songs during the week. The show starts, the DJs go through the normal pre-show announcements, and news from the week. The first couple of songs get played - BDP's "Criminal Minded," Public Enemy's "Rebel Without a Pause," and something by Kid N Play. I run upstairs to grab something to munch on while I lock in for these next 2 hours of nonstop Hip-Hop. Then it happens! I didn't catch this song from the beginning. I picked it up where Rakim says *so, I fell into the groove of the wax and I said, how could I move the crowd? First of all, ain't no mistakes allowed/here's the instruction, put it together it's simple, ain't it but quite clever!* I was floored by what I just heard. "Whoa! Who is that?" I heard the voice before, but I couldn't quite put my finger on where. The song goes on *Some of you've been trying to write rhymes for years/but weak ideas irritate my ears, is this the best that you can make? Cause, if not, and you got more, I'll wait.* Now I'm standing next to my speakers, boppin' back and forth listening intently. *So turn up the bass, it's better when it's loud…. Cause I like to move the crowd.* I lost it! My fist goes over my mouth as if I just watched MJ go baseline and dunk on Patrick Ewing! I have never heard anything like this before. After the song was over the DJs came on the air and said, "That was "Move the Crowd" by Eric B. & Rakim." I sat on my bed thinking about that song. I stopped the tape I was recording on and went back to listen again. "OH MY GOD," I thought. Wait, did I just stop in the middle of recording the radio show just to play this song again? Yes, I did! I was that mesmerized by what I heard. I wanted to hear more. I pick up the phone and call my mentor DJ K2 Sharp. "Yo K2, man! Please tell me you have that song by Eric B. & Rakim, "Move the Crowd." He nonchalantly says, *"Of course I have it, who else would have it but me?"* The next day I was sitting in his garage next to his DJ setup ready to jump into this album. I'm examining the album cover like it was a classic marvel comic. First song comes on….

Boom, Pap! Boom, Boom, Boom, Pap!

Boom, Boom Pap, Boom, Boom! *I ain't no Joke! I used to let the mic smoke, now I slam it when I'm done and make sure it's broke!*

I felt every word of those first few lines. I sat there in a trance, nodding to everything I was hearing. Rakim's style is like no other. He's smooth but rough, direct yet subtle, intelligent, and hardcore all at the same time. "My Melody" comes through with real hard drums and deep scratches as Rakim glides across the beat delivering powerful but rhythmic lines all throughout the song and chorus.

The title track "Paid in Full" was the fifth and final single released from this album. With the familiar break-beat as the drum track and a recognizable bassline, Rakim is *Thinking of a master plan, cause ain't nothing but sweat inside my hand.* I remember thinking, "How does he come up with these rhymes?" This was an amazing piece of art that would mold me into my Profound persona. I was deep into Hip-Hop as much as a 12 yr. old could be and after listening to this album I knew this is what I wanted to do - be an emcee. I've said many times in interviews over the years, "Rakim is the reason I chose to be an emcee. He's the reason I put time and effort into every line, every syllable, every detail of what I create." Thirty-five years later this album means so much more to me now that I'm older and have learned how to appreciate the mastery behind Rakim's cadence and content. Is this Eric B. & Rakim's best album? No, I wouldn't say that, but I will say it is one of Hip-Hop's most influential albums. Ask Nas! I'm sure Rakim is your favorite rapper's favorite rapper.

## CHAPTER NINETEEN
*The Predator* – Ice Cube / *The Chronic* – Dr. Dre
30 Years Later
Written by MC Till

I was in middle school sitting front in center in our school auditorium. I was looking up at a guest speaker that seemed like a pretty cool guy. Then, he started to tell us how we should not listen to certain rap artists and their albums. One such album that was on the naughty list was *Doggystyle* by Snoop Doggy Dogg. You can probably guess what this young teen did later that day after school. I listened to *Doggystyle!* But, that's not all. I also pulled out *The Predator* by Ice Cube and *The Chronic* by Dr. Dre. These were like my trinity of favorites as a kid, especially *The Predator* and *The Chronic*. I loved those albums. I think *The Predator* was probably one of, if not, my favorite albums as a kid. I couldn't get enough of that album. *The Chronic* wasn't too far behind.

Many labeled these albums as "Gangsta Rap." I have not liked that title for a long time. I still don't. It feels too small: too simple for what I now would understand as complex. As a kid, I just listened to the music and enjoyed it. From time to time I would catch a word, phrase, or skit that did not sit well with me. It came across as vulgar or misogynistic even if I did not know the meaning of those words. I felt it. But, for the most part, it was just dope music to me. As a parent, spouse, and human being on this planet for several decades now I hear the music differently. I have more context and "Gangsta Rap" just doesn't seem to do it justice. Some would call it denigrating. I'm not going to disagree. However, I think there is more there. To me, this music has always been thought provoking.

I remember the first time I heard "Just Don't Bite It" by NWA. Oh my goodness, if my dad ever found out about this! I would only play it really low or in my headphones to ensure no one else heard it. Was that denigrating to women? Yeah, I would say so. However, it also really challenged me. Maybe not so much back then, but as I got older. Why would anyone make that song and particularly that skit at the beginning? Why would any woman even be involved in it? It was nothing more than audio porn. Is there anything redeeming about that? How could I in good faith listen to something like this? Is this okay? Is it okay to watch a movie with a similar scene in it? That actually has visuals behind it. This skit is just audio. Does that make it any better? The music, however it is labeled, made me think and continues to all these decades later.

Ice Cube and *The Predator* especially made me think. Ice Cube has rapped and tweeted several lyrics and memes that are problematic to me as an adult. Yet, I cannot deny how positively informative his music was to me as a young tween. I remember track #3 on The Predator was a skit where the listener kept hearing this phrase "What scares us is I think we hear is violence" from what appears to be a white woman. Then, what appears to be a black woman responds and says that when we look at the statistics black people are the ones who should be afraid citing that black people are the ones being killed by the "Police, the KKK, skinheads." When Ice Cube was accused of being anti-Semetic on his groundbreaking album Death Certificate he defended his lyrics. "I'm not against Jews in either of those songs. I'm just doing what they do in the media. When they describe someone they often say he's black or Korean or Muslim. That's all I'm doing. Saying he's a Jew doesn't mean I don't like Jews or I'm using a negative. I don't like (Heller), but it's not because he's

Jewish." I won't justify his lyrics or memes in question. However, what Ice Cube and *The Predator* did for me was provide me with a different perspective. It was not always one I agreed with and let me assure you I take massive issue with many of his lyrics as I reflect. But again, it was not as simple as saying he is an evil gangsta rapper and that I should burn his CDs as some did in the '90s.

*The Chronic* by Dr. Dre played a similar complex role in my youthful development. On one hand it was an incredible piece of art. The production was some of the best ever up to that point and the lyrical skill especially of a young Snoop Dog was nearly flawless. On the other hand there were misogynistic lyrics, lyrics that degraded other men, violent lyrics and more. Surely these lyrics are not good for the betterment of society. Can't they in fact keep us from moving forward, inspiring people to do the very things they hear in the lyrics? I guess a lot of it depends on the ears that the music lands on. I remember taking a Psychology class in college. There was a study that the professor cited that concluded that aggressive violent music will not make an average person become aggressive and violent. However, if a person is already inclined to violence and if she or he is worked up and ready to be violent, the aggressive "gangsta rap" could be what pushes the person over the line to commit violence. When I hear problematic lyrics I don't respond violently or anything like that. I respond by thinking. Art is an invitation. The lyrical content is a launching pad for a myriad of questions (see the questions I posed in the second paragraph above).

And herein lies my challenge with art. It is not the same for each consumer. Each person uniquely experiences art. *The Predator* and *The Chronic* are two of the worst, most misogynistic, violent albums in history, says one listener. Another hails these albums as two innovative classics, pushing the boundaries of what art can and should be. I settle down somewhere in the middle. I hear both sides and I appreciate the arguments for both sides. For me these two albums and several like it have had a profound impact on me and I think it's for the better. They challenge me. They inspire me musically. But I also see the other side. I see why some would invite us to rethink if albums and art like this have enough redeeming qualities to praise them and their creators. For me the answer is yes and. Let us praise these albums when we hear praiseworthy material and critique them when they need critiquing. Let us not just simply say, "don't listen to this album or that" like our guest speaker did all those years ago. Instead, let us enter into dialogue around such albums. And so in the spirit of that kind of conversation, what do you think?

## CHAPTER TWENTY
*Bizarre Ride II the Pharcyde* – The Pharcyde
30 Years Later
Written by MC Till

I was reluctant, but I agreed. I would select and play 20 songs from Digable Planets during a Pharcyde vs Digable Planets song-for-song battle. Now I love Digable Planets and I think their sophomore album is better than The Pharcyde's sophomore effort. However, *Bizarre Ride to the Pharcyde* is a near masterpiece exuding with synergy, creativity, and innovation. Of the four albums that were allowed during the battle (first two from both groups) I was confident that Bizarre Ride was the far superior album. Even though Digable Planets somehow won that battle, I'm still convinced that The Pharcyde's debut is one of the greatest Hip-Hop albums of all time.

Musically it is perfect. It combines live instrumental interludes with sample heavy production for the 11 songs on the album. This combination of samples and instrumentation provides balance with just a touch of tension. It keeps us listeners on our toes. J-Swift, who did the majority of production, was amazing throughout. There is not a weak beat on this album. Musically it is filled with one high after another.

This was one reason I was reluctant to play the side of Digable Planets in that battle. A few months later I was asked to be part of a discussion around the samples found on *Bizarre Ride to the Pharcyde*. This wasn't a battle or anything like that. We simply found the samples via WhoSampled.com. We played the original sample and then played the Pharcyde song that utilized that sample. Oh, it was incredible as J-Swift perfectly used the technique of sampling on this album. I mean perfect.

One of my favorite samples on the album is on the opener, "Oh Sh*t." They use an extremely short part of "Beale Street" by Donald Byrd, but did they ever make that short sample sing. Another example is how J-Swift and the crew utilized a few samples from Stanley Cowell. The first is a piano sample which sets off the album along with a lovely saxophone. Those sounds quickly transition into what sounds like a vibraphone sample which is one of my favorite sounds over a boom bap beat. Of course I'd be remiss if I didn't mention "Passin Me By." The bass, the organ chops, the crackle of the vinyl, the drums: perfection. Oh and then that horn sample on the hook with Fatlip darn near screaming "She keeps on passin'" while the voice changes over to a smooth crooner for the second part of the line, "me by." The juxtaposition of that loud screaming voice and that super cool laid back voice captures the essence of this song. It is frustrating but also so beautiful. It is raw but also so smooth. It is how we live; in the tension of beauty and despair, of hope and apathy.

Cutting through the lackluster elements of our lives was their humor. The Pharcyde was fun and funny. A lot was happening in 1992 the year *Bizarre Ride* came out. Earlier in that year riots erupted in Los Angeles after four police officers were acquitted of violently beating Rodney King. That was no laughing matter. However, laughter can be a healing balm. The Pharcyde provided such healing. It wasn't just in their single "Ya Mama", an ode to playing the dozens, but also in how they formatted the album altogether. The album features a handful of 'skits.' Think of them less as skits and more as light hearted musical interludes. They made us feel like we were there, right there in the room jamming out to what felt like impromptu freestyles. Then of course we all were waiting and waiting on Quinton. I mean he was on the way and we were all for it. We couldn't wait. I believe Quinton got a deal off the strength of that skit alone! That's crazy if that's true.

What I do know is true is that *The Bizarre Ride II the Pharcyde* is a triumph in originality. It took chances and won. Its sampling was magnificent. It was humorous and light, providing comfort to the distressed. It was all this and more. It was and is a classic album in my book featuring one of the greatest Hip-Hop songs in "Passin' Me By." Sure I was happy that night because I won the battle playing all Digable Planets songs. However, if I was just listening and not playing the songs, my vote would have gone to the Pharcyde off the strength of their debut album alone.

## CHAPTER TWENTY-ONE
*Jewelz* – O.C.
25 Years Later
Written by MC Till

I can tell you exactly where I was when I first heard *Stakes is High* by De La Soul. I remember the Christmas morning when my brother gave me a Biz Markie tape. I know the bus ride I took with my senior high basketball team when I listened to *One Day it Will All Make Sense* by Common. But, for the life of me, I cannot recall when I first heard or when I first got my hands on *Jewelz* by O.C. I just know that shortly after it came out in 1997 I had the CD and it was amazing. Still is. What sticks out to me about this album is how good it was back then and how it seems to get even better over time. To say it has aged well is an understatement.

It begins like several albums of that era with a short intro beat. Even though it is less than a minute, it is not a throw-away beat. It is an invitation to the sound of the album. It has a serious tone which O.C. does too. It also contains an element of mysteriousness which to me is 100% O.C. from his voice to the way he puts his words together to his content. He reveals just enough to let us enter in and explore. Once in, it is hard to leave.

And here we are at the first song, "My World" where O.C. brings us into his world over an impeccable yet subtle sample from DJ Premier driven by what sounds like an old elder of the community whistling a melancholy melody. The very next track is "War Games", where DJ Premier gives us one of those standard Premo bangers. I love the piano sample in this beat. It stabs us on the 1, 2, and 3, and then opens up and flows into the

4 and then circles back. If you don't know what I mean, you'll just have to listen to the beat. The cherry on the top here is the guest feature on the hook - Pharoahe Monch and Prince Po of Organized Konfusion. To me this is a top tier hook. It is creative as they go back and forth and use different rhythmic patterns to draw the listener in. Everything about this song is darn near perfect.

That near perfection remains throughout the entire album. From the production side of things, why wouldn't it? Just look at this track rundown: 4 beats provided by DJ Premier, 3 by the Beatminerz, 2 by Buckwild, 2 by OGee (a much overlooked producer), 1 by Lord Finesse, and 1 by Mr. Walt. There is no possible way the production on any album with those names is going to be anything less than good. And let me assure you it is much better than good. Each producer provides some of their best beats of the era on *Jewelz*. That's the production. On the lyrical tip, come on, it's O.C. I mean just listen to his debut album, *Word is Life* and one instantly knows that this guy is cut from G.O.A.T. cloth. His flow is like no other. He manages to rhyme words that don't rhyme in ways that don't make sense but sound like they do. He is one of a kind and it is on full display here.

Also on display are several highlights. Honestly, the entire album is straight highlights. But I'll point out a few of my favorites:

"Dangerous" featuring Big L - Obviously Big L is always fun to hear. But what I love about this song is that it is my favorite use of the "Daisy Lady" sample. The Beatminerz knocked it out of the park on this one.

"Win the G" and "M.U.G" with guest Bumpy Knuckles, who then turns into Freddie Foxxx or maybe it is the opposite. They have great aggressive energy with two hard knocking Premo beats.

"Far From Yours" featuring Yvette Michele - Buckwild lays one of the most perfect instrumentals for O.C. to get down to. So lovely.

After so much incredible music we arrive at the final two songs which arguably are the best songs on the album! "It's Only Right" is a stripped down banger with the beat provided by Da Beatminerz. That bassline is beautiful and the underground drums are perfect. Then add OC just dancing around the beat and we have something truly amazing. Then we get this nice little vocal interlude that takes us back to what sounds like a park jam rooting the album to the foundation of Hip-Hop. Swiftly after that we get another of many short instrumental interludes before the final beat comes in with OC adding some introductory ad libs. He acknowledges his Diggin In The Crates crew specifically pointing out Lord Finesse who crafts the beat to this final song. This song ties a nice little bow on the entire album. It is once again a bit mysterious from OC's vocals to Lord Finesse's sampling choices. It is the perfect ending to a darn near perfect album.

I can't tell you exactly where I was when I first heard *Jewelz*. What I can tell you is that it found me. I'm thankful it did. This is one of my all time favorites and what's amazing is that even after all these years and after all the times I've listened to this album, I still find new gems with each listen.

## CHAPTER TWENTY-TWO
*Doom* - Mood
25 Years Later
Written MC Till

*Doom* by Mood is one of the best Hip-Hop albums ever. It has every ingredient for a classic boom bap project: great chemistry between two dope emcees, engaging lyricism, thoughtful content, raw yet crisp production, and a most cohesive consistent vibe throughout. The listener doesn't have to skip a track. They can turn it on, hit play, and let it ride.

I think it is fitting that such an amazing, yet underappreciated, album comes out of Cincinnati. Home to Scribble Jam for many years, Cincinnati's Hip-Hop scene is one of the best. It inspired Common to get his start in rapping, it helped propel battle rap legends such as Juice, Supernat, and a young, rather unknown Eminem. It catapulted Talib Kweli's career along with Mos Def. It birthed one of the greatest, yet unsung, Hip-Hop producers of our time in Hi-Tek. Cincinnati, and Ohio in general, was fertile ground for the rise in funk with King Records. Funk in return would provide much inspiration for the rest of the musical world including a more direct line to Hip-Hop. But does Cincinnati get its flowers in these regards? Not really. Not if you ask Cincinnati Hip-Hop artists. Many will tell you the city does not get her just dues.

So, let's at least give space to celebrate one of the great Hip-Hop albums of the '90s. Donte and Main Flow are the two emcees of the group. Talib Kweli stops by on several tracks. The production is handled primarily by Hi-Tek and Jahson. Let's start with the lyrical presence of the duo. They are perfect together. Their vocal tones and delivery styles amazingly compliment one another. They are similar enough to where if you like one, you'll like the other but different enough to where it never gets monotonous. Concerning the content, they delve into what some might describe as conspiracies. But their reporting is done in such a serious tone that they come across like in depth investigative reporters. What is reality, might not be. The listener is challenged to enter their world and learn. It is an easy entry too because the musical landscape that Hi-Tek and Jahson provide borders on the beautiful and the eerie. "Karma" is a near perfect Hip-Hop song with clean drums and an accenting sample. The next beat for "The Vision" is more mysterious with drums that are a bit more rugged. The very next beat on "Tunnel Bound" contains a perfect blend of that clean, crisp drum sound with a mysterious, eerie sounding sample. The entire album is like this and whether it is more rugged or smoother, the production doesn't falter for a second.

If you dig boom bap Hip-Hop from the mid-'90s, I don't see how you would not love this album. Similarly I'm not sure how anyone can experience the Cincinnati Hip-Hop scene and not gain an immediate appreciation for its brilliance. Donte, Main Flow, Jahson, and Hi-Tek are two emcees and two producers who are more than deserving of such appreciation. If you've heard *Doom,* give it another spin, post about it, tag the artists and show that love. If you've never heard the album, give it a spin. If it does not rise to one of your favorite albums of all time, I am confident you will still thoroughly appreciate its boom bap ingredients and enjoy them.

## CHAPTER TWENTY-THREE
*Fan-Tas-Tic Vol 1* – Slum Village
25 Years Later
Written by MC Till

Slum Village's second album featured Q-Tip, Kurrupt, D'Angelo, Pete Rock, Busta Rhymes, and Common. You have arguably the greatest Hip-Hop collective represented in the Native Tongues (Tip and Busta), one of the most influential West Coast labels ever in Death Row (Kurupt), arguably the greatest Hip-Hop producer ever in Pete Rock, and a "Neo Soul" boom bap, R&B, once-in-a-lifetime artist named Michael Archer, aka D'Angelo. This *Volume 2* album was endorsed by some of the greatest artists and movements of a classic Hip-Hop era. So can you imagine what kind of album preceded that? Something amazing.

*Volume 1* definitely was that. That album was and is an under-the-radar influential powerhouse. That album turned heads. You know that meme that circulated for a while where the guy was turned around checking out another woman while the woman he was with had that look of disgust on her face? That guy represents Hip-Hop producers back in the 90s who heard that *Volume 1* album by Slum Village or simply heard Jay Dilla's production. Producers had a way of making music and some of those early to mid-'90s beatsmiths made some classics. But they still turned their heads away from what they knew to fawn over Dilla and his new sound. They were mesmerized by Dilla's performance with artists such as The Pharcyde, Busta Rhymes, De La Soul, as well as *Volume 1*. Hence, why *Volume 2* has only legendary artists as guests. Think about that? Their "official" debut, *Volume 2*, only featured legendary artists and the music matched that legendary guest status.

But, I'm not here to talk solely about *Volume 2*, though it is helpful to know the context. That was their debut on a larger label with distribution. But before that, *Volume 1* is what got heads to turn and take notice of a Detroit trio named Slum Village. The crew was Baatin (RIP), Jay Dilla (RIP), and T3. All three were emcees while Dilla held down the double duty of rhyming and producing. It might be easy to fall into praising Dilla's production so much that we forget how dope Baatin and T3 were on that album. We also might not recognize Dilla's greatness on the mic that sometimes and I guess rightfully gets overshadowed by how amazing his beats were.

I've heard Hip-Hop heads say that Dilla was not a good emcee and that Baatin and T3 were not much better. I wholeheartedly disagree. I did not always appreciate what they talked about. I felt like they often lacked meaningful content, sometimes rhyming crass lyrics especially in how they addressed women. What I did appreciate about their mic presence is how creative they were. They took chances. Sometimes they would sound more professional like they had a decent mic and recording booth. Other times they would sound like they were rhyming into a microphone they found in a dumpster behind a kids toy store. Sometimes they would sound more polished, riding the beat in more traditional ways. Other times they had a staccato flow, pausing and going and pausing again. They seemed to relish in being original regardless of how it landed. They played by their own rules. All three of them fit this description, with T3 being a master of originality on the mic and Dilla being the master on the beats.

If I had to pick the greatest aspect of the album, I would definitely say the beats. I remember talking with my friend BTAM (RIP) about Dilla's production in the late '90s. One thing that he and I appreciated about Dilla's production was his snares. They were so loud and crackling and crisp, but also raw. Back in the 80's there is the infamous Marly Marl lost reel where he sampled a bunch of drum sounds on this particular reel-to-reel. He misplaced it. Whoever found it, started using those drum sounds and producers right and left followed suit by sampling those same drum sounds from Marly Marl. I think Dilla's drums were like that Marly Marl reel-to-reel. A lot of drum sounds since *Volume 1* all the way up to today can be traced back to Dilla. His deep, thumping kick drum, loud snare, hi-hats with light vinyl crackling can be recognized in many underground Hip-Hop beats. In addition to stellar drums, Dilla was a king of sampling. You can Google "Dilla Sampling" via YouTube and several videos will come up. Splice did a pretty good breakdown of Dilla and his sampling as did Vox. What strikes me about Dilla is that he was not a trained musician. He found his way to the MPC 3000 and made it his instrument. He studied it. He learned it. As Brain Radar Ellis puts it in the Vox video about Dilla, "He humanized the drum machine."

In a way you could say he helped humanize emceeing too. Along with T3 and Baatin he made rhyming sound so fresh, so down to earth, not wordy or intricate like many emcees of that era. It was this stylish presence on the mic that gave Dilla's amazing beats an extra layer of intrigue. I am confident that producers turned their heads when they heard Dilla's production. I suggest it wasn't just producers. I think emcees did too. I know I did. After hearing Slum Village, I wanted to be more accessible as an emcee. I wanted to sound like I was dancing around the beat, having fun, and worry less about being perfect. This off kilter style of rhyming and Dilla's humanizing of the drum machine was the perfect combination for an album that would go on to influence both emcees, producers, and underground fans alike.

## CHAPTER TWENTY-FOUR
*Power in Numbers* – Jurassic 5
20 Years Later
Written by MC Till

The night was Friday, May 13, 2005 and I had recently moved to Cincinnati. I didn't know anyone who wanted to go with me so I went solo. On my way there I slipped in Jurassic 5's *Quality Control* and turned it up loud. I arrived at the University of Cincinnati ready to see one of my favorite Hip-Hop groups perform live on campus at a free show. I thought I really liked Jurassic 5 before that night. I mean who can front on that album I played in the car ride there? And before that album they gave us that J5 Ep with songs like "Jayou" and "Concrete Schoolyard." Their most recent album at that point was *Power in Numbers* which we will get to in just one moment. But, I have to tell you what I saw that night in Cincinnati was not just a group of emcees and two DJ's making dope music. I saw the greatest Hip-Hop group show ever. I had never seen a group perform in such an engaging way up to that point and I have not seen one since. Not like that. Chali 2na, Akil, Soup, Marc 7 traded lines and movements while DJ Nu-Mark and Cut Chemist orchestrated the music like masters. Everything about that performance was just right from the movements to who said what when. They crescendoed, built energy out of thin air, dispersed it, brought it back: they were true masters of the ceremony. The audience ate it up and it was delicious.

That's kind of how I feel about their album *Power in Numbers*. This is a musical masterpiece. It begins with the perfect intro that's a mix of empowering words (not raps as we are just getting warmed up here) and a super funky bassline laying over an even funkier break beat driven drum bed. The final moment of the intro you hear someone say "This is Freedom" which goes right into the first song "Freedom." The pouding 1-2 of the kick and snare lays the heartbeat of the album. This album is all soul. I mean it is definitely a boom bap Hip-Hop album no doubt, but it is also a soul album. The soul disseminates out the speakers as we hear the sampled hook sing out *Hold on to this feeling. Freedom. Freedom.* We also hear very brief moments of this hook trying to make its way into the verses. It is almost as if freedom isn't free just yet, but it's near.

A few songs later we get hit with two of the funkiest J5 songs ever with "Break" and "A Day at the Races" with the latter featuring lyrical icons Big Daddy Kane and Percy P. Oh man, do these guys deliver. Both of them are on top of their game. Go listen to that song and sit in awe of their lyrical presence. And as dope as they are, it's not like they run laps around J5. Instead J5 holds their own and Chali 2na might just spit the best verse. I'll let you decide that.

The album is moving along at an alarming rate so what does J5 do next? They take that momentum and welcome you into storytime. Kind of reminiscent of Common's "I Used to Love Her." They are talking about a person but can't remember his name. Finally the very last thing you hear in the song is the name and it's not what you expect. It is a very clever song that deals with a pitfall in life. But then the very next song is an ode to living life to the fullest. On "What's Golden" they don't just live it up. They live it right. They celebrate living an honorable life, not one that chases after material wealth. It is dope. I'm telling you, soulful!

From here we get a good mixture of songs that have depth and songs that are just funky and dope. "Thin Line" deals with friendship and boundaries. "After School Program" is soulful to the 9th degree while "High Fidelity" features a dope, boom bap, sampled-based beat for top tier lyricists to flex their skills and styles. "Sum of Us" continues this formula to perfection adding in a little wisdom here and there. Again they have this really dope momentum similar to earlier in the album and what do they do this time? They drop out the music, feature an acapella Kool Keith verse, and transition into the darkest sounding song on the album, "One of Them" where they warn us of certain types of humans. It is an aggressive calling out of all that's phony. Before a final instrumental track J5 gives the silky soulful, "Hey," produced by Sa-Ra Creative Partners. These children of God allow J5 to show a softer side to give the album a little balance. The final vocal song is the very uplifting "I Am Somebody" followed by "Acetate Prophets," a six minute whirlwind through boom bap, sampled soul.

*Power in Numbers* masterfully uses momentum shifts to provide the listener with not just a fun listen, but an engaging ride. It features top tier lyricism, beats, uplifting messages, and a lot of soul. If you have never given this album a spin, I suggest you find it and give it a try. And if you have heard it and maybe it wasn't all that great to your ears, maybe give it another listen and see what happens. Maybe you won't be mesmerized like I was when I saw them perform live all those years ago. But perhaps you will hear something different that will spark your imagination or bring a smile to your soul.

# CHAPTER TWENTY-FIVE
*Blazing Arrow* - Blackalicious
20 Years Later
Written by Beau Brown

> *If nothing else I'll leave the world some songs that speak from the soul.*
> - Timothy "Gift of Gab" Parker on "Purest Love"

There are a select few albums that manage, at once, to be ahead of their time and perfect for the moment. N.W.A.'s *Straight Outta Compton*, Outkast's *Aquemini*, and Radiohead's *Kid A* all come to mind. Without a doubt, Blackalicious's second LP and major-label debut *Blazing Arrow* belongs in this category. Twenty years ago, Hip-Hop was at a very interesting inflection point. The first golden-age (mid-'90s) was about a half-decade in the rearview, and the rise of a new era of Southern artists like Lil Jon and Young Jeezy was beginning. In the midst of all this, a newer bifurcation was solidifying between underground and mainstream Hip-Hop. I keenly remember the attitudes of many erstwhile backpackers whose main activity was criticizing anything that sold more than a few thousand copies.

Yet, here was this funky duo from northern California that sounded decidedly underground, with the lyrical dexterity of Gift of Gab and the lush production of Chief Xcel, but was steadily gaining popularity outside the realm of purists. With their 2000 release Nia selling over 200,000 copies without a major label budget, Blackalicious was poised to gain a strange mixture of respect from the heads and a hearing with the masses. So, when MCA released Blazing Arrow in 2002, many questions were lingering. How did they use all that money? Would they sell out hunting for commercial success? Could they maintain the momentum they built with Nia?

After a first listen to this 74-minute album, the answer to the first question was relatively clear. They spent the MCA money on guests and production. For the time, it was a fairly star-studded lineup of artists from various genres. Well-known artists like Ben Harper, Gil Scott-Heron, ?uestlove, Ben Harper and Zack De La Rocha and lesser-known talent like Saul Williams, Lyrics Born, and Jaguar Wright all add flavor to the album without detracting from the overall sound. And the overall sound is beautiful. Orchestrated by Chief Xcel and recorded and mixed at top-notch studios, listening to all the layers and various arrangements on a pair of really good speakers is an incredible experience. With these guests and this sound, it was money well-spent.

On to the question of selling out. The quick and easy answer is, "No, I really don't think they did." A sellout album would not include a song like "Chemical Calisthenics," which is virtually inaccessible to the casual listener. A sellout album couldn't get by with an almost-ten-minute 3-part song with a spoken-word piece with phrases like *the pyramidic containment of an 'A'*. A sellout Hip-Hop album, in 2002, wouldn't include so much live instrumentation. By all accounts, Gab and Xcel made the album they wanted to make, and thankfully, the people at MCA gave them that freedom.

As far as maintaining their momentum…well, I guess it depends. Blackalicious certainly didn't become a runaway mainstream success. *Blazing Arrow* arrived at the previously-mentioned inflection point but did not immediately alter the sonic landscape of radio Hip-Hop. Despite the overwhelmingly positive critical reception of this album, it only spent 9 weeks on the Billboard Top 200 (compared to over 100 weeks for Lil Jon's *Kings of Crunk*). Their subsequent albums *The Craft* and *Imani Vol. 1* were dope, but they didn't reach the musical or commercial heights of *Blazing Arrow*. However, many of their Solesides/Quannum affiliates (DJ Shadow, Lyrics Born, Lifesavas, Pigeon John, etc) have consistently made positive impacts on Hip-Hop. And as I listen to more recent albums from younger artists like Kendrick Lamar's *To Pimp a Butterfly* or Black Milk's *Fever*, I can't help but wonder if *Blazing Arrow* has had a way more subtle (and way bigger) influence than I even realized.

It probably goes without saying that, along with many others, I deeply grieve the loss of Gift of Gab. He was not only an outstanding emcee, but as far as I can tell, he was just a humble, good dude, who loved to have fun and make music with his friends. He spoke from his soul, about things that really mattered, and he left an incredible legacy for all of us to appreciate and emulate. He left us way too soon, but the *Blazing Arrow* of his life will continue penetrating hearts and minds. Rest in Power, Timothy Jerome Parker. We are all grateful to you and Chief Xcel for this masterpiece.

## CHAPTER TWENTY-SIX
*Below the Heavens* – Blu & Exile
15 Years Later
Crowdsourced by MC Till

When something rises to the level of cult classic like *Below the Heavens* by Blu and Exile why not let the cult followers speak? That's what we decided to do with this album. We love the album and thought about writing a review for it, but decided to let you speak. So we put the word out on social media and asked, "What do you love about this album?" This is what we heard:

- Sequence, beats, rhymes and the life it gave. - Shawn Sawyer
- Classic album. The whole aesthetic and ambiance is so consistent and cohesive. - Zach Sternberg
- Everything - Michael Moose Campisi
- The raw honesty and transparency of an artist that's literally just trying to live. - Taj the Poet
- The production is flawless in my opinion and Blu just floats over it like it was made only for him. - Anthony L'Italien
- Same thing I like about all their albums. How they both compliment each other. The production and rhymes always go together seamlessly. - Rob Campbell
- The lyricism and content. - Terence Jordan
- Blu is dead nice. - Roger Folklorico
- Lyrics & Beats 👊👊👊 - Melvin Chavers II
- Absolute classic album, smooth beats and flow. Chill vibes. - Troy LaPointe

- Everything! Great memories with this album as 2008 was a happy eventful year and this was the soundtrack. - Michael Mantinaos
- Dope beats, dope rhymes. - Lex Pierre
- This is such an amazing album and I found out about it a few years too late and don't even remember any album that came out that year. I heard it because it was on repeat so much. It is an absolute classic!! - Simon Best
- It proved real Hip-Hop can come from anywhere !! - Joseph Greer III
- Beats, flow, rhymes. - Sonia Chatha
- Lyrics. - Msiematic Adamant
- I love literally everything about this album. My ears find no faults. Although I enjoy the other albums from them or the solo joints or Exiles production on anything, I always come back to this one. - Adam Joslin
- Flawless production that matched deep thought provoking lyrics 🎤🎤🎤🎤 - Jason Lynch Sr.
- Album is so fluent - Willie Beamen
- This is a perfect project. No misses. Closest thing to Moment of Truth I've heard. - Joseph Gargano
- It's the vibes 4 me. - Kevin McGlockton
- Everything. - Nor Senoj
- Blue Collar Worker! I love that song. I also love Exile's soulful, bouncy, funky production. Those beats tell a story all by themselves but don't sound too busy when Blu is doing his thing on top. They work so well together and everytime they make a project, I love it! - MC Till
- The whole vibe of this album is just right imo - Sean O'Neil

- I use this album as an introduction to the folks who haven't yet been blessed by this duo's mastery... and have yet to have any complaints. Front to back it's seamless yet disjointed enough to mimic life's ups and downs. One of my favorites. - Lucas Motejl
- The production is always a standout. - William Russ
- The cover - Jea M Ows

What about you? What do you love about this album? Hit us up and let us know!

# CHAPTER TWENTY-SEVEN
*Rap for Cure*
Written by MC Till

I remember the day like it was my worst. My wife had cancer. We found out that day. It was in May, 2012. How was I going to respond? How was my wife going to hold up? Would she go through chemotherapy? Would we forego modern medicine for a more natural approach? It was an anxious time. Somehow we managed to research and listen to several different doctors and family members and made the decision to do both a modern and natural approach. So chemotherapy would start in just a few weeks.

It was a lot to handle. Even though we did not have much money, I made the decision to not be a stickler on two things: my wife's health and mine. Part of my mental stability would come through music. I told myself that anytime I wanted to, I could drop by Everybody's Records and buy any CD I wanted. This might seem silly but when anxiety grips me, new music helps get it off. I get lost in the music and everything else around me falls silent. I needed some of that silence during those chemotherapy months. It was rough.

So, when friends and family came to visit and provided a break from being a full time nurse, husband, and father, I would zip over to the record store. The first few albums I found that summer would provide me an outlet for all my anxiety, frustration, and anger. I didn't want my wife to have cancer or go through chemotherapy but she did and was. I had to accept it. I did but with that acceptance came some upset feelings. Those feelings would linger around but would find a home in that first album I found, *Cancer for Cure,* by El-P. It is probably my least favorite El-P release but it did what it needed to do at the time. This album is filled with angst and anger, both in what he was rapping about and in the sound of the album. I needed that angry feeling. My anger needed an outlet and El-P provided just that.

Killer Mike pops up on track 6, "Tougher Colder Killer." Mike, along with that entire song, packed a punch. Hearing about death might not seem to be the thing that should bring comfort. But ironically it did. I did not realize that Camu Tao, friend and label mate of El-P's, died of lung cancer and this album *Cancer for Cure* is in large part El-P coming to grips with the reality of his death. Wow. When I realized this, it hit me. It sucks. And it is also beautiful how one person's pain or death can create another person's art. And that art can be therapy for countless people.

Killer Mike would reappear a few weeks later that summer. I was out on another run to Everybody's Records and Wil (someone who worked there at the time) grabbed an album from behind the counter. Someone had just turned in a used copy of *R.A.P. Music* by Killer Mike. As soon as I got in the car to head back home I threw the CD in the disc changer and instantly heard an aggressive Killer Mike rap, *Hardcore G sh\*t, homie, I don't play around...* He wasn't playing around on that first song nor was he playing on the next 11 songs. He teamed up with El-P to create what would become one of the most decade defining moments in Hip-Hop and maybe music in general. This was the beginning of Run the Jewels, a Hip-Hop group that can be seen rocking underground stages or performing hit songs on late night talk shows. They are everywhere. But that summer of 2012 they were just getting started.

*R.A.P. Music* is reminiscent of Ice Cube combining forces with the Bomb Squad or Kool G Rap linking up with Sir Jinx. El-P and Killer Mike. Who would have seen that coming? I sure didn't but I'm glad it came because that album not only helped me get through that chemotherapy summer but it inspired me way beyond that. Killer Mike is phenomenal on the mic. He is the killer of mics after all. He is ferocious, knows how to rap his butt off, and invites the listener to wrestle with all kinds of engaging and challenging ideas. Then there is El-P's original production. He knows how to inject personality into beats. These aren't smooth, laid back tracks to vibe to. They are sounds of madness that could be the soundtrack to riots: wild, sometimes dark, but always dope.

There were other albums that year of 2012 that helped me get through. Masta Ace gave us *MA_DOOM: Son of Yvonne* with beats sourced from the one and only MF DOOM. Sean Price blessed us with *Mic Tyson*. Brother Ali made what I think was his best album at the time with *Mourning in America*. *Reloaded* by Roc Marciano came out and one of my favorites to this day also came out called *Dice Game* by Guilty Simpson and Apollo Brown. Several dope albums dropped in 2012, but *Cancer for Cure* and *R.A.P. Music* are the two that most imprinted my angry and angst-filled existence that summer. Fitting. It would be Killer Mike and El-P that would go on to become one of the biggest pop sensations just a few years later. Thankfully I was able to watch that happen with my wife who has been cancer free ever since that summer. Chemotherapy was her cure. Rap was mine.

## CHAPTER TWENTY-EIGHT
*Return of the Don* – Kool G Rap
5 Years Later
Written by MC Till

Rakim is arguably the greatest emcee Hip-Hop has ever produced. Many believe he single-handedly elevated the art of rapping further than any other emcee before or since. Within a decade of Rakim's arrival, Hip-Hop was introduced to another prolific, game-changing emcee in Nas. It is not a stretch to say Nas took the torch from Rakim and elevated the art even further.

But, there were a few emcees in between Rakim & Nas who were also upper echelon emcees. Kool G Rap was one of them. In fact Def Jam records passed on signing Nas in the early '90s because Russell Simons thought he sounded too much like Kool G Rap. In other words one of the greatest emcees in the world got shot down because a decision was made that he wasn't better than Kool G Rap. Probably the wrong decision, but still it is not crazy to put Kool G Rap in the list of greatest emcees of all time.

Five years ago he gave us another reason to call him great with *Return of the Don,* produced entirely by MoSS. One producer at the helm gives the listener a really great, cohesive sound. Nothing seems out of place here. And although MoSS doesn't break through with something amazing on this album, he doesn't disappoint either. His production is straightforward; sample heavy with an emphasis on soul and grit. This simple formula works well as Kool G Rap muses about street life, criminal activity, and the like. The album is called *Return of the Don* after all. The content is not for the faint at heart.

Even if the listener doesn't go for the Mafioso street tales of the criminal underworld, he or she can still enjoy elements of this album. Kool G Rap remains prolific in his ability to rhyme within the bar and to utilize multisyllabic rhymes. Even when he is not saying anything really incredible he is saying it in an incredible way. It is always enjoyable to listen to. Just as MoSS doesn't give us anything earth shattering on the beats, Kool G Rap doesn't personally break new ground on the mic. Still, the level at which he was rhyming on *Return* was light-years beyond just about every other emcee releasing music back in 2017.

And in the essence of a Don, Kool G Rap brings in other emcees to carry the lyrical load. In several songs Kool G Rap spits the first verse and then the guest emcees do the rest of the work. I can just see him in the booth doing his thing and then sitting back with a drink in one hand, cigar in the other, and his feet propped up on the coffee table. But don't worry. While he's relaxing, the guest emcees are cooking up something tasty. A few highlights include AG Da Coroner, Raekwon, Saigon, and Lil Fame. Sean Price is featured with Ransom on "Popped Off", leaving us a bit melancholy. Stealing the show on the features for me is Conway and Westside Gunn. They are the last two voices you hear on the project. And they don't really say anything incredible, but they say it in a very engaging and compelling way. Maybe Kool G Rap featured them last for a reason. Maybe it was a subtle endorsement and reassurance that the future of grimy Hip-Hop was in good hands.

I don't think *Return of the Don* is a masterpiece or even a classic album. But, it is a good piece of art that further solidifies Kool G Rap's place as one of the greatest to ever do it. And thankfully he's not done yet. It is amazing that Kool G Rap is lyrically superior to almost every emcee that has come out since his debut release in 1989. Sure, some have elevated rap to new levels. But, most fall short of the intricate skills that Kool G Rap possesses. In a culture where too many living legends release irrelevant music or none at all it is refreshing that a Hip-Hop veteran 30+ years into the game, can still come correct. Kool G Rap probably won't move up the ranks in the greatest emcees of all time lists with this album. But, he won't move down either. He will remain and that alone is more than impressive.

Part Five
# THE PEOPLE'S LISTS

## Fhaez's Favorites

*Trees* - Avantdale Bowling Club
*Guidelinez* - Capone & Dillinger
*Cheat Codes* - Dangermouse & Black Thought
*Intros, Outros & Interlude's* - Domo Genesis & Evidence
*Live From The End Of The World Vol. 1* - Fatlip & Blu
*Wolve's Don't Eat With Shepherd's* - Knowledge The Pirate & Big Ghost Ltd
*Flying High* - LMD
*Magic* - Nas
*Glorious Definitely* - Nelson Dialect & Must Volkoff
*Forever* - Phife Dawg

## Ismail Ghedamsi-filion's Top 20 English Albums

1. *The Menu* - Leaf Dog & BVA
2. *Nicest Emcee* - C-keys
3. *Bring Me Back When The World Is Cured* - Sadistik
4. *Cavalcade of Cosmic Crips and Interplanetary Pirus* - Murs & Rob Viktum
5. *Blabberastic Semantics* - BlabberMouf & Sneadr
6. *The Sundown EP* - Freddie Marr and Th.iii.rd
7. *The Haymaker* - Faf
8. *Esoteric-sanctimony* - Keggles Mc
9. *Acres of Diamonds* - ILL Conscious x Mute Won
10. *Cheat Codes* - black thought
11. *Lupe Fiasco* - DRILL MUSIC IN ZION
12. *Determination* - Termanology
13. *Digital Damage* - Emma Beko
14. *Harsh-livin* - Hazz
15. *TAKU SNI* - Bazille
16. *Spektah Revisited* - Ghostown
17. *Even In Death* - Cubbiebear x Seez Mics
18. *Renaissance Kings* - Snowgoons
19. *Maison de Medici* - Napoleon Da Legend
20. *Composed* - Rob Gonzales

## Ismail Ghedamsi-filion's Favorite Non-English Hip-Hop Albums

*Time Flies At Light Speed* - Lerics Dalyricist
*Sangue Nero* - Odiopuro
*A Luta Continua* - Lucha Amada
*Placebo Society* - Samanos
*MISTAGRAM* - MISTAGRAM

# Some Final Words

The day was November 8th. It was the day we were supposed to submit our book to be edited. Well, one week earlier my life would be forever turned upside down. My daughter woke up to the flickering lights of multiple police cars outside of our house. It was around 4:30 a.m. Six cars in all. Then an ambulance. Then a firetruck. Later a crime scene unit van and plain clothed officers filling out forms. Later that night my wife would be sitting down with one of the daughters who just lost their dad while I sat down with a stepson who was trying to process what just happened. How would he "step up" for his mom? Without putting all of their business out there, they lost a husband and father that morning in pretty traumatic fashion. Everything else in my life felt instantly insignificant. I couldn't imagine what that kind of loss felt like. The weight of it all must be unbearable.

I had to speak at a Unitarian Universalist Church a few days after that. It was helpful. I spoke about my journey in and out of faith and in again. After I spoke, the congregation sang a final song. It was "Imagine" by John Lennon. I had heard the song before but being such a Hip-Hop head it wasn't a song I knew really well. But those lyrics and the feeling of the song and the way the musician played it that morning touched my soul. There is a line in the song that goes, *nothing to kill*. That phrase reached out of the air and grabbed me. I felt the sound waves encompass me.

I have seen the horror that gun violence causes. When I first moved to Cincinnati I was involved in a mentorship program at Woodward High School where Hi-Tek attended and graduated from. A teenager was shot and killed at a Shell gas station right around the corner one morning while kids were picking up snacks for the day.

Later, I worked in the computer lab at an elementary school a few miles down the street. One weekend a 1st grade student found a gun in the home and played with it. He did not come to school that Monday or any day after that. The bullet from the gun ended his life.

I moved on to another school, Frederick Douglass Elementary where I met one of the most caring people in the world. Her husband walked to the store one night. During the walk a fight broke out. Someone pulled a gun and shot at another person. The bullet hit the woman's husband. He played no part in the fight. He was just walking to the store. He never walked again. A bullet ended his life too.

Countless people have countless stories like this and it is always heartbreaking. The family in my neighborhood across the street is dealing with a very traumatic death experience. We are dealing with it. I think about the faces of his kids and how sad they looked. I think about the face of the woman who lost her husband. I think about that first grade teacher's face on that Monday. I think about the teenagers' faces who saw their classmate gunned down. These faces are not okay. They should be smiling and filled with joy instead of looks of terror, unparalleled pain, fear, confusion, and more.

*Nothing to kill.* I want nothing to kill. I want life. For all of us. And I want music to reflect that. I want boom bap Hip-Hop that has nothing and no one to kill. Instead I want Hip-Hop music to uplift and inspire.

I know that life can be hard. Terribly traumatic things happen. Art needs to reflect those feelings and give meaning to those emotions. But can we, as artists, do it in such a way that promotes? Can we enter into the pain of loss with compassion and hope? Art is important. It is necessary not for our survival as people, but for our ability to thrive and build community together. That's the boom bap Hip-Hop I want to hear. And that's the music I want to promote.

May we all love others and be loved.

Peace,
MC Till

Before we get out of here, we want to say thank you to all our patreon supporters:

Marek Parda
Brandon Baker
Christopher Nurnberger
Donn Calloway
Charlie Johnson
Adam Condron
Beau Brown
Fhaez
Ismail Ghedamsi-filion
jeffrey alan
Cayce Harris
Peter Zeleznik
Sara Hayden
Dug Boogie
Mark Thomson
Yapheth Tesfai
StarFire Teja Ray Shankara
Anne Brack
Adrian Nicotra
Mark A. Harris
Wally Hart
Ben Polinsky
dee.kay
Matthew Phillips
Andrew Whitton
Myrtis Smith
John Stickney
Taylor Hogle
Joe Thomas
Who Izzy

If you like what you see in this book, then become a part of it! Sign up at **patreon.com/everybodyshiphop** today!

See what we are up to at **www.everybodyshiphop.com**